HISTORY OF THE MASS

IS VOLUME
110
OF THE

Twentieth Century Encyclopedia of Catholicism

UNDER SECTION
X
THE WORSHIP OF THE CHURCH

IT IS ALSO THE

9TH
VOLUME IN ORDER OF PUBLICATION

Edited by HENRI DANIEL-ROPS of the Académie Française

HISTORY OF THE MASS

By *FRANÇOIS AMIOT*

Translated from the French by LANCELOT C. SHEPPARD

HAWTHORN BOOKS · PUBLISHERS · *New York*

First Edition, January, 1959

NIHIL OBSTAT

Johannes M. T. Barton, S.T.D., L.S.S.

   Censor Deputatus

IMPRIMATUR

E. Morrogh Bernard

   Vicarius Generalis

Westmonasterii, die XI SEPTEMBRIS MCMLVIII

2 8 2
E 5 6
V. 110

BX 2230
A 533
Cop. 2

The Library of Congress has catalogued this publication as follows:

Amiot, François.
   History of the Mass. Translated from the French by Lancelot C. Sheppard. [1st ed.] New York, Hawthorn Books [1959]

   141 p. 21 cm. (The Twentieth century encyclopedia of Catholicism, v. 110. Section 10: The worship of the church)

   Bibliography: p. [140]–141.

---

   1. Mass—Hist.   (Series: The Twentieth century encyclopedia of Catholicism, v. 110)

BX2230.A533   264.025   59–6668

CONTENTS

FOREWORD

This is the body which is to be given up for you: this is
the cup of the new testament, in my blood, says the Lord:
do this whenever you drink it for a commemoration of
me.

(Communion for the first Sunday in Passiontide.)

Pius XII, in the encyclical *Mediator Dei et hominum* of
November 20th, 1947, defines the sacred liturgy as "the public
worship which our Redeemer as Head of the Church renders
to the heavenly Father as well as the worship which the community of the faithful renders to its Founder, and through
him to the heavenly Father. It is, in short, the worship rendered by the mystical Body of Christ in the entirety of its
Head and of its members".

This definition, full as it is of profound doctrine, is of
supreme value when applied to the Mass; for the Mass is the
very sacrifice of Jesus Christ himself, an extension of the
sacrifice of Calvary, offered by the ministry of the Church.
The invisible offering of Christ is made manifest by the action
of the Church, especially at the consecration, by which he
becomes present on the altar in the perfection of those dispositions which filled his heart on the cross and won the
redemption of the world. The worship offered by Christ to the
Father, the worship offered to Christ and to the Father by
the Church, are inseparable; it is in the Mass that they find
their most perfect expression.

The Mass is the centre of divine worship, of the homage rendered to God by the Church: it is the Church's prayer *par excellence*, Christ's prayer offered by the Church to God, the perfect praise and thanksgiving, the unique source of the divine gifts and graces of redemption, especially for those who participate in it completely by eucharistic communion.

The Church has chosen to surround this essential act of her worship with ceremonies and prayers, in order that it may be performed by her children with the supreme reverence it demands, enlightened by faith and with abundant fruitfulness. She has provided for this both in the preparatory prayers and readings as well as in the specifically sacrificial liturgy, with the communion and the concluding thanksgiving. It is this assemblage of venerable formularies and actions that the present volume is concerned to examine in the light of history. They are deserving of our full attention by reason of their antiquity, beauty and their doctrinal and sanctifying power. The development they have undergone during the course of the centuries will enable us to acquire a better understanding of their significance and to unite ourselves to them more profitably.

*   *   *

The nature of the present series forbids any display of erudition. Critical apparatus has therefore been reduced to a minimum. On the other hand, the aim has been to omit nothing essential and to avoid oversimplification. It has not always been possible to give detailed proofs in support of the solutions proposed for certain obscure problems. The reader need not on that account lose confidence; if he wishes to embark upon a more profound study, he can refer to the bibliography at the end of the book. Nothing has been said about oriental liturgies (which form the subject of another volume in this series) except in so far as they provide helpful comparisons and facilitate an understanding of the Roman Mass.[1]

The translations of the liturgical text are taken whenever possible from *The Missal in Latin and English* by Fr J. O'Connell and Mr H. P. R. Finberg.[2]

[1] In this connection see particularly *Comparative Liturgy* by Anton Baumstark, listed in the Select Bibliography at the end of this book.

[2] Burns and Oates, London, and Newman Press, Westminster, Md, 1957.

CHAPTER I

A GLANCE AT ORIGINS

THE LAST SUPPER

The Mass is the repetition of the Last Supper in the course of which Christ delivered to his apostles the mysteries of his body and blood, thus preparing for the bloody sacrifice of Calvary. The oldest account of the Supper, earlier than the Gospels of SS. Matthew, Mark and Luke, is that given by St Paul in 1 Corinthians (11. 23–9) written at Ephesus in the spring of 55 or 56:

> The tradition which I received from the Lord, and handed on to you, is that the Lord Jesus, on the night when he was being betrayed, took bread, and gave thanks, and broke it, and said, Take, eat; this is my body, given up for you. Do this for a commemoration of me. And so with the cup, when supper was ended, This cup, he said, is the new testament, in my blood. Do this, whenever you drink it, for a commemoration of me. So it is the Lord's death that you are heralding, whenever you eat this bread and drink this cup, until he comes; and therefore, if anyone eats this bread or drinks this cup of the Lord unworthily, he will be held to account for the Lord's body and blood. A man must examine himself first, and then eat of that bread and drink of that cup; he is eating and drinking damnation to himself if he eats and drinks unworthily, not recognizing the Lord's body for what it is.

This ancient account is rich in doctrine. It connects the Eucharist very closely with the passion. A new and permanent alliance is concluded between God and man in the blood of Jesus. His immolation was mystically anticipated at the Last

Supper. The command is given to the apostles, and implicitly to their successors, to celebrate the Eucharist in his memory; and this remembrance is of such efficacy that it is an unceasing proclamation of his redemptive death and in a certain manner renders it actually present, until the day when Christ returns in the full glory of his second coming. Finally, great purity of soul is required to take part in a rite as sacred as the reception of the body and blood of the Lord.

St Luke's account is very similar, as one might expect from the disciple and companion of St Paul. It clearly includes the Eucharist in the paschal meal. St Matthew and St Mark give a slightly different formula for the chalice: "This is my blood of the new testament." They do not postpone the giving of the chalice until after the supper; the two consecrations are placed side by side and no mention is made of any interval between them, just as the discipline of the Church was soon to require; the supper already seems to have been relegated to a position of secondary importance and was soon to disappear altogether.

ST JUSTIN

On the other hand, the divine praise or thanksgiving which St Paul mentions and which derives from the Jewish ritual, developed and acquired such prominence that the entire celebration was often termed the Eucharist. We possess a characteristic example of this, although its eucharistic application is not certain, in the ninth and tenth chapters of the *Didache* or *Doctrine of the Apostles*, a valuable little treatise from the first half of the second century. Another element, sacred readings accompanied by the singing of psalms, borrowed from the Sabbath service of the synagogue, was not long in establishing the connection between the religion of the Jews and Christianity and took its place as an introductory prelude to the actual offering of the eucharistic sacrifice. This evolution is already clear in the famous description which St Justin gives, in about 150, in chapters 65–7 of his *First Apology*. He

begins by speaking of the eucharistic liturgy of the newly
baptized, and then proceeds to describe the Sunday liturgy:

After having thus baptized him that is persuaded and has
given his assent, we bring him to where the brethren, as they
are called, are gathered together, that we may make earnest
prayers in common both for ourselves and for the newly enlightened, and for all others everywhere, with the express
intention that, having come to the knowledge of the truth, we
may be worthy to live piously a life of good works and keep
the commandments, so that we may obtain eternal salvation.
Having recited these prayers, we salute each other with a kiss.
Then is brought to the president of the brethren bread and a
cup of water and wine. He takes them and offers up praise and
glory to the Father of the universe through the name of the
Son and of the Holy Spirit, and makes thanksgiving at length
for our having been vouchsafed these things from him. And
when he has finished the prayers and the thanksgiving, the
whole people present responds, saying "Amen". Now "Amen"
in the Hebrew language signifies "So be it". And after the
president has given thanks and the whole people responded,
those who with us are called deacons give to each of those
present to partake of the bread and wine and water which has
been made Eucharist, and to those who are absent they carry
away [portions].

And this food is called by us Eucharist; and it is not lawful
for anyone to partake of it but him who believes our teaching
to be true, and has been washed with the washing which is for
the forgiveness of sins and unto a new birth, and who so lives
as Christ commanded. For not as common bread or common
drink do we receive these things, but just as Jesus Christ, our
Saviour, being made flesh through the word of God, took both
flesh and blood for our salvation, so also we have been taught
that the food which has been made Eucharist by the word of
prayer that comes from him, by which [food] our blood and
flesh by conversion are nourished, is both flesh and blood of
that Jesus who was made flesh. For the apostles in the memoirs
which they composed, which are called Gospels, have thus
related that the command was given to them: That Jesus,
having taken bread and given thanks, said "Do this in remem-

brance of me: this is my body"; and having taken the cup likewise and given thanks, he said: "This is my blood" and he gave it to them alone. And the evil demons imitating this have commanded it to be done also in the mysteries of Mithras; for that bread and a cup of water are set forth with certain formularies in their rites of initiation, you either know or can learn.

And afterwards henceforth we continually put each other in mind of these things; and those of us who are well off help those who are in want; and we always consort together. And for all things that we eat we bless the Maker of all through his Son, Jesus Christ, and through the Holy Spirit. And on what is called the day of the Sun there is a meeting of all who live in cities or the country; and the memoirs of the apostles or the writings of the prophets are read as long as time allows. Then when the reader has ceased, the president gives by word of mouth his admonition and exhortation to imitate these good things. Afterwards we all rise up together and offer prayers; and, as I said, when we have ceased to pray, bread is brought and wine and water, and the president likewise offers up prayers and thanksgivings to the best of his power; and the people respond with "Amen". Then follows the distribution to each and the partaking of the things which have been made Eucharist; and to those who are absent [a portion] is sent by the hands of the deacons. Of those who are well-to-do and willing, everyone gives what he will according to his own purpose; and what is collected is deposited with the president; and he it is that succours orphans and widows and those who are in want through sickness or any other cause, and those who are in bonds, and the strangers who are in need. Now we hold our common meeting on the day of the Sun because it is the first day, on which God changed the darkness and matter in his making of the world, and Jesus Christ, our Saviour, on the same day rose from the dead. For on the day before Saturn's they crucified him, and on the day after, which is the day of the Sun, he appeared to his apostles and disciples and taught them these things, which also we have put before you for your consideration.

The interest of this description is obvious. It reveals the chief features of the eucharistic service: readings from the Old

Testament, a reading from the "Memoirs of the Apostles" or "Gospels" (it is the first time this name occurs in early Christian writings), then a homily and prayers, the offering of bread and of wine mixed with water by means of a formula in which the idea of thanksgiving (Eucharist) predominates, then communion and the sending of the Eucharist by the deacons to those who are absent. The assembly associates itself with the president by acclamations and at the end by its offerings for the poor, but not, apparently, by bringing bread and wine to the altar. Belief in the real presence of the body and blood of Christ in the consecrated elements is clearly stated. Finally, it is on the day of the Sun, Sunday, that the liturgy is celebrated in memory of our Lord's resurrection.

THE ANAPHORA OF ST HIPPOLYTUS

Illuminating as it is on many points, the Apology of St Justin does not give us any text of the formulas then in use, no doubt because they were improvised by the celebrant who "offered up prayers and thanksgivings to the best of his power". This freedom lasted for a long time; but we may suppose that the more solemn prayers would have been carefully prepared in advance and in most cases would not have been left to chance or the inspiration of the moment. In any case, several ancient texts have come down to us, and they throw considerable light on the primitive character of what we call the Canon of the Mass, the central prayer which enshrines the consecration. In ancient times such prayers were termed "anaphora", from two Greek words meaning lifting on high, offering. We give here that of St Hippolytus, a Roman priest whose ambition led him to become an antipope, but who was later reconciled to the Church and died a martyr in 235. It is taken from his tract *The Apostolic Tradition*, where it is inserted after the prayer for the consecration of a bishop:

May the Lord be with you; and let all say: And with thy spirit. Lift up your hearts: We have lifted them up to the Lord.

Let us give thanks to the Lord. It is right and just. And so let him continue: We render thanks unto thee, O God, through thy beloved Child, Jesus Christ, whom in the last times thou hast sent to us, a Saviour and Redeemer and the Messenger of thy will; who is thy Word inseparable, through whom thou hast created all things and in whom thou wast well pleased; whom thou didst send from heaven into the Virgin's womb and who, being conceived, was made flesh and was shown to be thy Son, being born of the Holy Spirit and a Virgin; who, fulfilling thy will and preparing for thee a holy people, stretched forth his hands when he suffered that he might deliver from suffering those who have believed in thee.

Who when he was betrayed to voluntary suffering that he might abolish death and break the bonds of the devil and tread down hell and enlighten the just and establish the testament and manifest the resurrection, taking bread and giving thanks to thee, said: Take, eat; this is my body which is broken for you. Likewise also the cup, saying: This is my blood which is shed for you; when you do this, you make remembrance of me.

Mindful, therefore, of his death and resurrection, we offer thee the bread and the cup, giving thanks to thee that thou hast found us worthy to stand before thee and minister to thee. And we pray that thou wouldst send thy Holy Spirit upon the oblation of holy Church; in gathering them together in unity, that thou wouldst grant to all the saints who partake that they may be filled with the Holy Spirit for the strengthening of their faith in truth, so that we may praise and glorify thee through thy Child, Jesus Christ, through whom glory and honour is unto thee, the Father and Son with the Holy Spirit, in thy Holy Church, both now and for ages unending. Amen.

The reader will have no difficulty in recognizing in this anaphora a simple and pure form of the general lines of the present canon of the Mass, leaving out the *Sanctus* and the Mementos. After the initial dialogue of the Preface there comes the thanksgiving for the incarnation of the Son of God and his passion. There follows a mention of the fruits of the passion and then the account of the Last Supper. Finally, there is the declaration that the Church is acting in obedience

to our Saviour's command in making remembrance both of
his death and of his resurrection, and in offering the consecrated bread and wine. Consequently, she asks God to send
the Holy Spirit upon her offering so that her children may be
strengthened in their faith and unending praise may be offered
through Jesus Christ to the adorable Trinity. Everything, or
nearly everything, is said with a few lines: the sacrifice of
Calvary is commemorated, the Church's offering is united to
that of Christ, the prevailing thought is of praise and thanksgiving for the redemptive mystery which is perpetuated on the
altar and for the glorifying of the Trinity.

THE DE SACRAMENTIS

From the middle of the third century and especially after
the Edict of Milan (A.D. 313), which marked the end of the
first persecutions, both formularies and ceremonies began to
develop not only in the fore-Mass with its intercessory prayers
for the Church but also in the anaphora itself. The liturgies
of east and west[1] began to vary, the latter being characterized
by a much greater variety of formularies in the course of the
liturgical year. In the Roman liturgy Latin was gradually substituted for Greek, and the fore-Mass and the other variable
parts were systematically arranged, while the canon began to
resemble its present form. Towards the end of the fourth
century St Ambrose of Milan, in a collection of instructions
for the newly baptized entitled *De Sacramentis*, quotes the
central part of the canon, which is substantially identical with,
though somewhat shorter than, the text of our missal.[2] Before
long the other prayers of the present canon were added, and
it seems probable that Pope Gelasius (492–6) gave the canon
its complete form; only the memento of the dead was lacking
and this was added later.

[1] See Jungmann, *The Mass of the Roman Rite*, I, pp. 33–7, for the
anaphoras of Serapion, Bishop of Thmuis in Egypt, and of the *Apostolic Constitutions*; both go back to the fourth century.

[2] Text in Jungmann, *op. cit.*

THE SACRAMENTARIES

The prayers said by the celebrant, which (apart from the canon) are all variable, have come down to us in small books called sacramentaries (*Liber Sacramentorum, Sacramentorium*). Three of these, the Leonine, the Gelasian and the Gregorian, contain the Roman Mass.

The Leonine sacramentary is not an official compilation. It seems to date from about 540, but it contains a number of texts which by their style and doctrinal value justify us in attributing it to St Leo (440–61). We possess only a single manuscript, dating from the seventh century, and this unfortunately is incomplete; it lacks the Masses from Christmas to the middle of April. Nearly two hundred formularies of our missal come from this sacramentary. It contains a surprising number of Masses in honour of famous saints such as St Lawrence and SS. Peter and Paul.

The Gelasian sacramentary cannot be attributed with certainty to Gelasius (492–6), except perhaps for the general order of certain formularies. It has an official value and has come down to us in its oldest form in a manuscript dating from the beginning of the eighth century. It gives in order the Masses of Christmastime and Easter, then those of the saints, and finally the Sunday Masses with the canon and several votive Masses. Many Gallican elements are incorporated; those of Roman origin date from the sixth century at latest. There is another type of Gelasian sacramentary which is represented by many manuscripts; this is the Frankish Gelasian, or the Gelasian of the eighth century, which contains Gregorian elements.

The Gregorian sacramentary derives in its present form from the copy (it has unfortunately been lost) which Pope Adrian sent to Charlemagne at his request in 785 or 786. This original was the work of St Gregory and the study of comparative liturgy has enabled us to recover its main lines. The manuscripts we possess are not older than the ninth century;

they contain a number of ancient Roman elements together with Gallican elements added by Alcuin. The primitive text, being designed for solemn papal Masses, did not contain the Masses of ordinary Sundays. Alcuin took these from the Gelasian sacramentary and made many additions to them suited to the Gallican temperament, of a rather more lyrical and imaginative nature than the sober genius of Rome. This supplement ended by being included in the Roman books.

In addition to the sacramentaries there were in the early days lectionaries for the Epistle and Gospels and antiphonaries for the parts chanted by the schola. Little by little the habit grew for the celebrant to read those parts of the Mass which were not especially set apart for him, and in the Middle Ages this led to the compilation of a *Missale plenarium*, a complete Missal and the ancestor of our Roman Missal, uniting in a single book the contents of sacramentary, lectionary and antiphonary.

THE ORDINES ROMANI

Finally we must mention the *Ordines Romani* which describe in detail the order of the papal Mass and provide an indispensable complement to the liturgical texts. We possess a complete series reaching from the seventh to the fourteenth centuries, some of which describe the bishop's Mass. The most important is that one published by Mabillon under the title of *Ordo Romanus I*; it dates from the end of the seventh century. It is this text which forms our chief guide in describing the Roman Mass during the period of St Gregory, a period of particular importance in the evolution of the liturgy.

The word "Mass", by which we designate the essential act of divine worship together with the rites and prayers which enshrine it, has a very unexpected etymology. It comes from the Latin *missa* which means dismissal. At the end of the fore-Mass, or the preparatory part, there was the dismissal of the catechumens (candidates for baptism) and sometimes also of the public penitents. When the holy sacrifice was over, the rest of the gathering were in their turn dismissed—this being the second dismissal or *missa*, from which the name Mass was given to the whole celebration; and sometimes in the Latin texts we find *missarum solemnia* in the plural, the solemn ceremony of the dismissals. This name Mass, taken from a very obvious external rite, ultimately prevailed in the west. It is true that it might at first have had a deeper significance: in those days they were more conscious of how baptism and the whole effect of Christian initiation set the faithful quite apart by making them members of the Church and demanded that when the celebration of the sacred mysteries began those who had not yet received this initiation or who had rendered themselves unworthy of it should be dismissed. Nevertheless, it is a matter for regret that some of the more ancient expressions have fallen out of use, expressions which were full of savour and significance: the Breaking of Bread (taken from the Acts of the Apostles), the Synaxis or assembly, the Lord's Supper, the Eucharist, the Liturgy or divine service *par excellence*, the Oblation, the Communion, the holy Sacrifice. Only this last is still retained in frequent use.

CHAPTER II

THE PAPAL MASS IN ST. GREGORY'S DAY

The pontificate of St Gregory (590–604) is important for many reasons, especially as regards the order of divine worship. Everyone knows that it is to this great pope that we owe the Church's traditional chant. But it is not so well known that, apart from minor additions and amplifications, it was he who gave the Mass its definitive form. It is a matter of great interest to see how Mass was celebrated in his day and in the subsequent period, up to the end of the seventh century, by studying *Ordo Romanus I*. It is not a question of studying the past in order to imitate it—such archeological methods are expressly condemned in Pius XII's Encyclical. No, the study of ancient rites must have as its object the acquiring of a clearer and deeper knowledge of the Mass as we have it, by setting in relief its essential features upon which our understanding and our devotion should be especially focused.

The pope came on horseback in solemn procession from the Lateran, accompanied by the clergy who were to assist him. On days of penance he made his way first of all to another church in which took place the *collecta*, or gathering of the faithful; from there they went in procession, singing the litany of the saints, to the station church,[1] where the pope would celebrate Mass. On other days the pontifical procession went straight to the station church where the people were

[1] In Rome to this day Mass is still celebrated during Lent in the same stational churches as in St Gregory's time.

assembled. In the *secretarium* (or sacristy) the pope and his ministers donned their sacred vestments. Meanwhile, an acolyte accompanied by a subdeacon carried the book of the Gospels to the altar. When all was ready the pope entered the church to the singing of the introit, preceded by seven acolytes with their lighted torches and the thurifers, and escorted by seven deacons. When he arrived at the altar he was presented with a portion of the *Sancta*, bread consecrated at a previous Mass, which he venerated by bowing before it. He then gave the kiss of peace to a bishop, to a priest and to the deacons. Having prostrated himself on a carpet for a short silent prayer, he kissed the altar and the book of the Gospels and signed to the schola to bring the introit to an end.

During the singing of the *Kyrie* the pope proceeded to his throne which was placed behind the altar at the furthest point of the apse. He prayed facing eastwards, so that if the apse was at the west end of the church he would turn towards the people and if it was at the east end he would turn his back on them. Arrived at his throne, he brought the *Kyrie* to an end and intoned the *Gloria* if it was to be sung. When this was finished the pontiff greeted the assembly and chanted the Collect or prayer.

After this splendid prelude there came what we may term the office of lessons (or readings). A subdeacon went up into an ambo (or pulpit) and read the Epistle. He was followed by a member of the schola who, alternately with the singers, performed the gradual and the other intervening chants, which provided an element of relaxation and meditation. The Gospel, the last of the readings, was naturally surrounded with the greatest solemnity. The deacon begged the pope's blessing, kissed the book which had been placed on the altar and went to the ambo, preceded by the thurifer and two torches. When he had finished reading, a subdeacon invited the clergy to kiss the sacred text. Sometimes there was a homily after the Gospel. Apparently by this time the dismissal or *missa* of the catechumens had dropped out of use.

Once again the pope greeted the congregation and added *Oremus*, but this was no longer followed by a prayer. Immediately acolytes and deacons spread a cloth on the altar, hitherto uncovered, and there followed the offertory. At the entrance to the nave the pope, together with the archdeacon, received the offerings of the nobles, while one of his assistants or one of the other clerics did the same for the people. Meanwhile the schola sang the offertory psalm. When the offertory was finished, the pope, after washing his hands, left his throne and went to the altar. There he placed his personal offering beside the loaves and the chalice to be consecrated, brought by the archdeacon. He then recited the secret, which at this period was the only prayer of offering.

The offertory, in which everybody took part, was a striking demonstration of religious unity between clergy and people. This became even more clearly marked when the pope was standing at the altar, surrounded by his assistants and nearer to the faithful. Everybody was now about to associate himself most closely with the prayer of consecration which the pontiff immediately began.

As in the preceding centuries, this prayer took the form of a thanksgiving: it was Eucharist in the Greek sense of the word. The Latins preferred the word Preface, which did not in any way signify a prelude, but a formula uttered before an assembly: *prae fari, praefatio*, a solemn prayer. It began with the very ancient dialogue of the *Sursum corda*, which introduced a prayer of praise and thanksgiving: *Gratias agamus* ... *Vere dignum et justum est* ... *semper et ubique gratias agere*. This prayer is an act of homage and gratitude to God for the benefits of the redemption, in which is inserted an account of the Last Supper and which ends with a doxology,[1] *omnis honor et gloria*, a worthy pendant to the initial *vere dignum*. The entire prayer has come to be known as the canon, or rule, on account of its practically invariable character. Its general

[1] The technical name for a formula of praise addressed to the three Persons of the blessed Trinity.

lines are the same today, lacking only in those days the
elevation and, as we have already noted, the memento of the
dead.

Behind him the pope had the bishops, priests and deacons;
the subdeacons faced him on the other side of the altar with
their backs to the faithful. He said the words of the canon
aloud, including the consecration which was not yet marked
by any special rite. When he came to the final doxology, the
archdeacon lifted up the chalice, taking it by the handles
which he held with a linen cloth; in this way he indicated the
solemn conclusion of the anaphora.

The Lord's Prayer and the *Libera* which followed it began
the preparation for communion. It was St Gregory himself
who fixed the Lord's Prayer in its present place immediately
after the canon. The pope then gave the kiss of peace to his
assistants who gave it to the clergy and then to the people—
an exceedingly apt expression of unity and Christian charity
—before receiving the body and blood of Christ. It was now
necessary to proceed with the fraction, for in those days
ordinary loaves were consecrated. The pope began by breaking off a fragment of the host, leaving it on a paten on the
altar, and returned to his throne. The archdeacon placed the
chalice on the right hand, leaving it in the charge of a subdeacon. He put the consecrated hosts into linen bags which
the acolytes held suspended round their necks. These then
went to the bishops, priests and deacons, and to them was
entrusted the breaking of the other loaves. This very important
rite took a certain amount of time and in St Gregory's day
it was performed in silence. In the next century, under Pope
Sergius, it was accompanied by the singing of the *Agnus Dei*.
During the fraction, curiously enough, the functionaries of the
pontifical court asked the pope for the names of the notables
he desired to entertain at the repast that was to follow, and
at once issued his invitations.[1] Communion followed, accom-

---

[1] Was this perhaps a survival of the fraternal repast or agape which
concluded originally with the Eucharist?

panied by the singing of a psalm, just on the same pattern as the introit and the offertory.

The fragment of consecrated bread which he had left on the altar was now brought to the pope. He divided it, putting one portion into the chalice and receiving the other; then the archdeacon offered him the chalice from which he took a little of the consecrated wine. The bishops, priests and deacons then came and received communion from the pope under the form of bread and the archdeacon gave them the precious blood. It was then the turn of the faithful. The pope left his throne and himself communicated the nobles, the archdeacon giving them the chalice. On his way back to the throne he gave communion to the lesser ministers. The ordinary folk were ministered to by the priests and deacons; those who did not communicate might withdraw. The Eucharist was received standing, in the right hand placed over the left, and women had their hand covered with a cloth. Each person thus gave himself communion under the form of bread, and then from a chalice proffered by a deacon took through a tube a little of the consecrated wine. The custom of communion under one kind was already developing.

When everything was ended the pope returned to the altar and recited a prayer of thanksgiving, or postcommunion. A deacon dismissed the congregation with *Ite missa est.* The pope retired in procession, blessing clergy and people as he went.

It is easy to find in our present Mass the same order as in this ancient Mass, though some of the later additions are lacking. These extra ceremonies and prayers are concerned with three moments in the liturgical action: the beginning, before going up to the altar; the offertory, in which there are more prayers for the offering of the bread and wine; the communion, where both in preparation and in thanksgiving additions have been made.[1] It is sufficient to imagine our Mass

[1] A comparison with other liturgies, especially those of the east, is of great interest here.

without these later elements to discover the Gregorian Mass almost exactly as it was. A contemporary of St Gregory who witnessed a solemn pontifical Mass today would not be seriously puzzled if he were given a few words of explanation. Perhaps he might wish for a more marked and a more obvious participation in the sacrifice by common prayer and general communion, essential features which came to be somewhat obscured but which the liturgical revival is now happily aiming to restore.

CHAPTER III

GENERAL PLAN

Among the plenary Missals already mentioned the thirteenth-century Missal of the Roman Curia is of particular importance not only on account of its origin but also because its use was widely spread by the Franciscans. Yet this Missal did not prevent a very great variety of ceremonies and formularies in the Mass-liturgy during the course of the Middle Ages. Our present Missal was the work of a commission appointed by Pius IV according to the express wish of the Council of Trent; the work was completed under his successor, St Pius V. The Missal of St Pius V was published and made obligatory on July 14th, 1570; only those religious orders or dioceses which possessed a liturgy of more than two hundred years' standing were allowed to keep their own. Thanks to the invention of printing, Pius V's Missal brought about a unification that nearly everybody desired. Its basis was the Missal of the Roman Curia. The modifications introduced by Clement VII and Urban VIII, then by St Pius X, made practically no changes in the text of the ordinary of the Mass and the canon, nor in the rites and ceremonies; they consisted mainly in alterations in the calendar, the introduction of new feasts and modifications of the rubrics. The Missals authorized by the French bishops during the seventeenth and eighteenth centuries only differed from the Roman Missal in proper parts of the Mass; they did not survive the return to the Roman liturgy which was effected during the course of the nineteenth century, chiefly under the influence of Dom Guéranger. So was brought to an end an over-exaggerated diversity (nearly every diocese had its own liturgy) with all its very obvious inconveniences. It must be agreed, however, that the reform was too radical and that it ought to have been possible to preserve at least some of the very beautiful and occasionally ancient texts, of the proses in particular, which certain dioceses have obtained leave from the Holy See to retain in part.

Anyone who takes the trouble to examine a Latin Missal can read in its first pages the Bull of Pius V, the Briefs of Clement VIII and Urban VIII and the Constitution of Pius X. He will find in the next place the calendar, the general rubrics with the corrections introduced as the result of Pius X's reform and the rites to be observed in the celebration of Mass. This latter section is a detailed and very precise description drawn up by Burchard, pontifical master of ceremonies at the beginning of the sixteenth century who was later raised to the episcopate; it owed much to the ancient *Ordines Romani.* Then follow instructions on the defects that may occur in the celebration of Mass. The Missal itself, properly speaking, begins with the prayers of preparation and thanksgiving, for the most part optional, after which it gives the Masses of the season, i.e. of the Sundays, of Lent and of the greater festivals. The ordinary of the Mass is by custom inserted between the Easter Vigil and the Mass of Easter—sometimes at the end of the Sundays after Pentecost. The Proper of the Season is followed by the special Masses for the feasts of saints (the Proper of the Saints) and then the Common of the Saints for those feasts which have not special Masses. In conclusion there are the votive Masses, various prayers (most of them very beautiful) and Masses for the dead. Often there are added certain appendices containing blessings and Masses proper to the diocese or religious order for which the Missal is destined. The whole constitutes an invaluable treasury; it will be our endeavour to call attention to some of the riches it contains.

Even a cursory examination of the ordinary of the Mass is enough to reveal its basic plan.

The fore-Mass, or Mass of the catechumens, is clearly distinct from the Mass properly so-called, the Mass of the faithful, which begins with the offertory.

The fore-Mass is made up of a prelude which takes us as far as the Collect and service of readings. This prelude is a straightforward service of praise, prayer and instruction. It includes:

the *Confiteor*, an act of contrition and repentance;
the *Kyrie*, a prayer of desire and intercession;
the *Gloria*, a hymn of praise;
the *collect*, a solemn prayer of petition which concludes the preceding prayers.

God replies, so to speak, to our prayer by the teaching which his word gives us: here we worship God by listening to the lessons. The various elements are as follows:

the Epistle;
the intervening chants, mostly from the psalms;
the Gospel, the last and most solemn reading;
on certain days, a sermon usually commenting on the lessons;
the profession of faith in the *Credo* completes the service.

After this spiritual and intellectual preparation the Church can offer the sacrifice of Christ. In this, the Mass properly so-called, we can easily distinguish three parts:

1. The offertory, or preparation of the sacrifice. The bread and wine are brought to the altar and offered to God in a service of rites and prayers which ends with the prayer known as the secret.

2. The consecration, or sacrifice properly so-called. Our gifts become the body and blood of Christ in the course of the great eucharistic prayer, which includes the preface and the canon.

3. Finally, in the communion, we receive back our gifts, now transformed by God's power, and with them divine life. This sacrificial banquet includes a preparation (the Lord's

Prayer, fraction, kiss of peace, prayers before communion), the act of communion, thanksgiving (postcommunion, dismissal, blessing and the concluding prayers).

This setting of the eucharistic sacrifice is not without complexity. If we are to understand the Mass we must pick out its essential features which are to some extent obscured by adventitious elements; and although these last are not without their value, we must realize that they are of secondary importance. The new *Ordo* for Holy Week seems in any case to herald further simplification.

A detailed examination of the Mass in the light of its history can only bring an increase of true piety; it will emphasize the continuity of tradition and its theological and religious value, and it will help us to participate with greater understanding and profit in the sacrifice of the altar.

CHAPTER IV

THE FORE-MASS :
THE INITIAL PRAYERS

We are not concerned here with the *collecta*, a gathering of the faithful in a church other than that in which Mass was to be celebrated, which took place in Rome on days of penance. On such occasions there was an introit followed by a prayer, and then a procession to the stational church,[1] during which the litanies were sung; Mass was celebrated in the stational church. On Sundays and feastdays the pope went straight to the church where he was to officiate. It is with this case that we are at present concerned.

THE PRAYERS AT THE FOOT OF THE ALTAR

We have already seen that at the time of St Gregory the pope came in procession to the altar and then prostrated himself in silent prayer for only a short while before going to his throne. An exactly similar silent prostration is still prescribed in the Good Friday office. From the eleventh century we find various rites of preparation.

Before vesting, the pontiff recited some of the penitential psalms, the number varying: at present five are appointed to be said and a bishop must recite them when he celebrates solemnly, but their recitation is optional for him on other

[1] The word "station" meant a military outpost in a foreign country. A Christian is a soldier of Christ and the Church adopted the word to indicate a gathering in an appointed church where the pope was to celebrate Mass.

occasions and always for ordinary priests. At the same period the processional entry and arrival at the altar were accompanied, especially in Frankish churches, by the recitation of *apologiae*, or prayers of confession, in which the celebrant avowed his unworthiness and asked pardon for his faults. Such prayers included the *Judica* psalm, the *Confiteor* (said twice in turn, as today), and then an absolution with versicles and prayers including *Aufer a nobis* which is still in use. Innocent III inserted all these in the Missal of the Roman Curia, and St Pius V later made them obligatory. Apparently until the twelfth century they were said on the way to the altar. It may be that the modern practice of dialogue Mass gives them too much emphasis; they are private prayers and it is paradoxical to make them an occasion for the greatest possible degree of participation on the part of the faithful. Sometimes, which is even more absurd, this dialogue is maintained at a sung Mass and at a time when the introit ought to be sung.

Since the fourteenth century the celebrant has begun with the solemn sign of the cross and the formula *In nomine Patris* which recalls that of the baptismal rite and in some way connects baptism with the Eucharist. It is a splendid act of faith, a sign of belonging to Christ. The bond between the two sacraments is even more marked by the sprinkling with holy water which normally precedes the chief Sunday Mass, accompanied by the singing of the *Asperges me* (in Paschal time, the *Vidi aquam*). This is a visible reminder of our baptism and of the necessity of purification from the stains of our post-baptismal sins.

The psalm *Judica me* follows at once, introduced and concluded by its fourth verse, *Introibo*; this singularly happy choice gives a joyful character to the fine psalm in which we express our ardent desire to enter the temple of God and to praise him, and thus to be protected from our powerful foes. During Passiontide the psalm itself is omitted and only its refrain retained, doubtless because the same psalm serves as

introit for the first Sunday of Passiontide. A similar omission
is made during the following days and at Requiem Masses.
The versicle *Adjutorium*, an appeal for divine help which is
used frequently in the Roman liturgy, introduces the *Confiteor*.

The alternate *Confiteor* is obviously penitential. First the
priest, and then his assistants, acknowledge their sins, beg
pardon for them and ask one another's prayers. In its rather
long present form it goes back to the Middle Ages. It evokes
the picture of the judgement in which the sinner accuses himself in the presence of God and his more illustrious saints,
and then of intercession in which he appeals for their mediation. The *Indulgentiam* is a deprecatory form of absolution
which for an appreciable time seems to have been considered
as sacramental, at least for the assistants (obviously the priest
could not absolve himself); nowadays it is clear that it in-
volves no sacramental intention, but the sentiments of repentance implied by the formula can obtain pardon for venial sin.

A few verses from the psalms and the *Dominus vobiscum*
are added to the *Confiteor*, and then the priest goes up to the
altar saying the beautiful prayer *Aufer a nobis*, an ancient
collect from the Leonine sacramentary. It is a further petition
for pardon before entering the holy of holies of the eucharistic
sacrifice, completing the transition between the world and
the sanctuary, a transition to which all these preliminary
prayers are directed.

The first action of the celebrant on arriving at the altar is
to kiss it with reverence. Since the thirteenth century this
kissing of the altar has been a frequent action at Mass.
Originally it was done in silence, as it still is on Good Friday
after the initial prostration. But here, in accordance with the
natural tendency to accompany an action with a prayer, the
priest says *Oramus te*, a comparatively late prayer (eleventh
or twelfth century), to judge by the fact that it is in the
singular, for all the ancient formulas are in the plural. It
expresses homage to the relics encased in the altar-stone, but

also to Christ himself, symbolized by the altar. The kiss is, as it were, the Church kissing Christ, accepting the union effected by his sacrifice. At pontifical Mass the bishop also kisses the text of the Gospel which the subdeacon carries before him during the procession and which, it will be remembered, he used formerly to place on the altar with the assistance of an acolyte, before the solemn entry. The custom, prescribed by the rubrics and still preserved in some dioceses, whereby the server at low Mass carries the Missal to the altar in front of the celebrant, is an interesting reminder of the ancient rite. Similarly, the veneration of the *Sancta* on arriving at the altar is still continued when the bishop pays a brief visit to the Blessed Sacrament chapel before going to the high altar to celebrate Mass.

At this point, since the eleventh century, there has been the rite of incensation of the cross and the altar, a rite which has not been introduced into Requiem Masses, which have only a limited solemnity. The use of incense in Mosaic worship is well known. The Romans used to carry incense before the consuls; later they did the same for bishops. From this derived the custom of incensing persons and things, especially the altar upon which the sacred mysteries were to be performed; the altar thus received a further mark of reverence and respect.

THE INTROIT

It is possible that originally, at least at stational Masses, the entrance procession took place in silence, as is still done on Good Friday. If so, the effect must have been somewhat austere, and for that reason at quite an early period greater solemnity was obtained by the addition of singing. This may have been introduced as far back as the fifth century, although apparently it was not until the sixth that the chant took the antiphonal form of a psalm with a refrain or antiphon repeated after each verse, or group of verses, sung by two choirs. In stational Masses, which were preceded by a procession with the singing of the litanies, there was no need for an introit;

hence there is none for the Mass of the Easter Vigil. Later on,
however, it was introduced into these Masses, such as that of
the Purification, Ash Wednesday and Palm Sunday.

Gradually the custom arose of not singing the introit until
the ministers had arrived at the altar, especially when the
distance from the sacristy was short. The Vatican *Graduale*
reacts against this error and indicates that the introit ought
to be sung during the procession to the altar. The new *Ordo*
of Holy Week requires that for the Mass of Maundy Thursday the procession should follow a long enough route for the
singers to chant several verses of the psalm and to repeat the
antiphon several times.

Owing to the fact that in most churches the entry procession
had become very short, the psalm was reduced to a single
verse with the *Gloria Patri*[1]; we shall see later that at the
offertory and communion the psalm disappeared completely,
leaving only the antiphon.

The shortening of the psalm must have had something to
do with the melodic elaboration of the antiphon which seems
to have taken place since the tenth century at least. Such
ornate melodies could obviously only be sung by the schola;
but the people could still have joined in the psalm-verse and
the doxology. These introit melodies are remarkable for their
solemnity and variety and the extraordinarily supple manner
in which the words are set. There is an abundance of masterpieces; almost at random we can cite the austere *Ad te levavi*
for the first Sunday of Advent, the joyful *Gaudete* for the
third Sunday, the exultant *Puer natus est* for the third Mass
of Christmas, the *Domine ne longe facias* for Palm Sunday, at
once sad and confident, the *Resurrexi* of Easter with its calm
serenity, the triumphant *Viri Galilaei* for the Ascension, the
broad and majestic *Spiritus Domini* for Pentecost. It would be
easy to multiply examples. We have here an inestimable
treasure, both musical and spiritual.

[1] This doxology originated in the east and began as a protestation
against the errors of Arianism.

The antiphon is normally taken from the psalm which it enshrines as in the Christmas midnight Mass, the Sundays of Lent and many other Masses. From the first to the seventeenth Sunday after Pentecost roughly speaking the order of the psalter is followed, beginning with psalm 12. Often enough the text comes from other books of the Bible, quoted more or less freely; the Prophets (Christmas Day, St John the Baptist), Epistle of the Mass (third Sunday of Advent, Ascension, St Peter), the Gospel (Vigils of St John the Baptist and St Peter); more rarely it is of the Church's own composition— technically known as ecclesiastical compositions—(*Gaudeamus* of All Saints, *Salve sancta parens* in Masses of our Lady); *Requiem aeternam* in Masses for the dead is adapted from the apocryphal fourth book of Esdras.

The introit is, as it were, the overture to the drama: it announces the mystery or the feast just as does the invitatory at Matins, but at greater length, suggesting an idea which contributes to an understanding of the Mass and indicating its supernatural intention. The fact that it is sung is excellent psychology and calls to mind the function of the chorus in ancient tragedy. The combination of words and melody is conducive to meditation. It has been finely compared to a triumphal arch at the end of a Roman road. Sometimes the introit has given its name to the Mass or even to the day itself —*Gaudete*, *Laetare* or *Quasimodo*, for instance.

We make the sign of the cross at the beginning of the introit because it marks the real beginning of the Mass. Nowadays the celebrant is required to recite it, like the other parts which are to be read or sung, but are not specifically reserved to him. It seems that this is an unfortunate instance of the influence of low Mass upon high Mass, as the result of which the priest seems to cut himself off from the assembly which it is his function to lead. Also, when the plenary Missals appeared, it may have been thought that everything contained in them was to be recited. Or again, it may have resulted from the celebration of Mass in vast churches in which it was impossible to hear easily. The recent *Ordo* for Holy Week directs that the celebrant should listen to the readings, and thus inaugurates a reaction against this state of affairs. But even if it were brought to an end, we may wonder whether many celebrants might not continue to read at least with their eyes all the texts of the Missal for often, in spite of the modern use of microphones, it is not easy to hear on account of the poor enunciation of many readers.

THE KYRIE ELEISON

The *Kyrie* is of eastern origin and was maintained in Greek probably by Pope Gelasius; it originated perhaps in Jerusalem. At first it was the response to a litany; to each invocation or intention for prayer formulated by the deacon the people answered *Kyrie eleison*, "Lord have mercy".[1] The adoption of the *Kyrie* at Mass seems to have coincided with the abolition of the prayer for the various needs of the Church, or *Oratio fidelium*, which occurred at the offertory and served a similar purpose. It is characteristic of the Good Friday service which begins with the lessons and has no *Kyrie* that it should have kept the solemn collects after the reading of the Passion. The invocations to which the *Kyrie* served as response at first disappeared on the ordinary days and then on the more solemn ones at about the time of St Gregory. When Mass was preceded by a procession with a litany there was no reason for the *Kyrie*; even nowadays at the Easter Vigil the *Kyrie* which concludes the litany serves also as that of the Mass. *Christe eleison* is of Roman origin.

The number of invocations was not at first laid down. The pope gave a sign to the singers to stop when he arrived at his throne. The threefold repetition of the threefold *Kyrie* (or

[1] An example of this form of prayer, probably due to Gelasius, will be found in Jungmann, *op. cit.*, I, pp. 336–7. The Byzantine liturgy of St John Chrysostom includes three litanies which are dialogues between the deacon and the faithful. Other oriental liturgies at this point exhibit a complex series of prayers and chants.

nine invocations in all) was first fixed in Gaul. Originally all were addressed to Christ; *Kyrios* is the special title given to him in Christian antiquity, particularly in St Paul. Increasingly, since the Middle Ages, a Trinitarian significance has been given to the *Kyrie*, each group of invocations being addressed successively to the three divine Persons. This development appears clearly in the farced *Kyrie* in which words (or tropes) were adapted to the long neums set to a single syllable[1]; the first words of these tropes have been retained in the Vatican Gradual as the names of the various Masses.[2] The trope formed possibly a useful mnemonic by which the melodies could be remembered but it was an obvious accretion which the Missal of St Pius V (1570) was fully justified in abolishing.

The melodies were developed particularly after the tenth century and our Gradual has preserved a considerable selection of them, several of which are very beautiful. *Lux et origo* (I) for Eastertide breathes the freshness and joy of spring, *Cunctipotens* (IV) displays a discreet archaism, *Cum jubilo* (IX) for Masses of our Lady is full of tender devotion; *Orbis factor* (XI) for ordinary Sundays is redolent of ardent supplication and *Deus Genitor* (XVIII) gives an impression of monastic simplicity. One of the most popular Masses everywhere is probably that known as *de Angelis* (VIII) on account of its more modern tonality.

The singing of the *Kyrie* and the other parts of the Ordinary of the Mass (*Gloria, Credo, Sanctus, Agnus Dei*) should be carried out by the congregation alternating with the choir, except, of course, when polyphonic Masses are sung. It is a great pity for all the singing to be reserved to the choir and

---

[1] For example, the first *Kyrie* of the Mass for use in Eastertide was farced thus: *Lux et origo lucis, summe Deus, eleison: Kyrie eleison.* Here the rhythm follows the melody; in others, as Jungmann (*op cit.*, I, 344) points out, a definite verse form (e.g. the hexameter) is used. [*Trans.*]

[2] Thus Mass I is called *Lux et origo* from the trope quoted above. [*Trans.*]

for the nave to be condemned to silence. The melodies are comparatively simple and a restricted repertoire will be amply sufficient for the needs of most congregations. It is essential that the participation of Christ's faithful—the congregation— in the public worship of the Church should not be confined to the few short responses in answer to the celebrant's salutations.

The *Kyrie* expresses our need of salvation and the genuine Christian desire for the coming of Christ, here and now, in the Eucharist and in the various means of grace and on the last day in glory. It is a suitable preparation for the collect in which the priest sets before God through Christ the prayer of the assembled Church. As it is in Greek it can also be regarded as a prayer for unity, and if it is remembered that it is the only remaining part of a litany it will act as an inspiration to pray, as we sing it, for all the members of the Church, the hierarchy, catechumens, sinners etc., and for all those important intentions that ceaselessly we bring before God, the sanctification of souls, the spread of the faith, the peace of the world.

THE GLORIA IN EXCELSIS

The *Gloria* is a beautiful trinitarian doxology which begins with the hymn of the angels at Bethlehem; it continues with exclamations of praise first to the Father, then to the only-begotten Son, exalts his godhead, implores his pardon and his glory. It concludes with a short reference to the Holy Spirit. Some authorities regret that the *Gloria* separates the *Kyrie* from the collect which formed the usual conclusion of the litany, but it bears a close relationship to it with its short invocations. In any case, it would be a great pity to deprive the Missal of this jewel of Christian antiquity.

The *Gloria* is a very ancient hymn of Greek origin (its rhythm is better in Greek than in Latin), one of the rare Christian psalms that have come down to us. In this category three others may be mentioned—*Te decet laus* said at Matins in the monastic Breviary, the *Te Deum* and the beautiful evening prayer of the Byzantine liturgy, "Joyous light". We possess different versions of the *Gloria*[1]; our western text is derived from that found in the *Codex Alexandrinus* after the New Testament. The following is a translation of the Latin version in the Missal:

> Glory be to God on high, and on earth peace to men of good will. We praise thee, we bless thee, we adore thee, we glorify thee, we give thee thanks for thy great glory. Lord God, heavenly King, God the almighty Father. Lord Jesus Christ, only-begotten Son. Lord God, Lamb of God, Son of the Father, who takest away the sins of the world, have mercy upon us; thou who takest away the sins of the world, receive our prayers; thou who sittest at the right hand of the Father, have mercy upon us. For thou alone art the Holy One. Thou alone art Lord. Thou, Jesus Christ, alone art the Most High, with the Holy Ghost, in the glory of God the Father. Amen.

The theological interest of the text is obvious and it repays detailed analysis.[2] Its lyrical quality is one of its attractive features; it is a joyful answer to the supplication of the *Kyrie*, and is the song of the redeemed who proclaim the greatness of God and of Christ and with an eager confidence implore a share in the graces of redemption.

In the early Church the *Gloria* was not said at Mass, but it soon found its way into the Christmas midnight Mass. Pope Symmachus extended its use to Sundays and the feasts of martyrs, but only at pontifical Masses. In the ninth century priests could say it only on Easter night and on taking possession of their church which, at Rome, followed immediately after ordination. Since the eleventh century priests can say it on the same days as bishops, that is, on all feasts of saints and on all Sundays except those in penitential seasons. The

---

[1] The Syrian version from the Nestorian liturgy, the Greek version in the *Apostolic Constitutions* and the Greek version from the Byzantine liturgy which is similar to that of the Roman Missal. Comparison of the two first will be found in Jungmann, *op. cit.*, I, 347–8. [*Trans.*]

[2] Such an analysis will be found in Jungmann, *op. cit.*, I, pp. 348–55.

only Masses at which it is omitted are those of the Sundays of Advent and Lent, ferial days throughout the year and at private (i.e. non-solemn) votive Masses.

The *Gloria* chants of Masses I, IV, VIII, IX and XI in the gradual possess the same musical qualities as the *Kyrie* to which they correspond and it is likewise proper for the congregation to take part in the singing. Attention may be drawn to *Gloria* XV (for simple feasts) which is a syllabic chant that is relatively unknown; its sober musical theme with its echo of church bells (like the first phrase of the *Te Deum*) produces, when sung by a large congregation, an extraordinary impression of power. The Christian community should sing the *Gloria* with all the ardour of its faith and love.

THE COLLECT

The *Gloria* or the *Kyrie*, according to circumstances, is followed by the greeting *Dominus vobiscum* ("The Lord be with you"), which throughout the Mass usually preceded the collects and directions given to the congregation. It is a gracious wish which sums up the whole of Christian life and is to some extent the equivalent of the Hebrew word Emmanuel, God with us. The priest says it with hands extended after kissing the altar, so to say thus taking Christ in order to give him to the faithful. It is a sober, moving and profound gesture entirely in accord with the restrained poetical note characteristic of the Roman rite. The congregation's answer *Et cum spiritu tuo* might well be regarded as a Semitism meaning "and with you". Nevertheless many prefer the more literal, and apparently less clear, "and with your spirit", for it is understood to contain doctrinal undertones: the spirit is not only what is inmost in the human soul but, according to an idea familiar to St Paul, is the soul raised up and supernaturalized by the presence of the Holy Spirit. Thus by a specifically Christian wish closely related to the life of grace answer is made to the priest's equally Christian greeting. At this point in the Mass a bishop says *Pax vobis*—

"Peace be with you". This was the risen Christ's greeting to
the apostles. It is said by a bishop at Masses which contain
the *Gloria*, no doubt in allusion to *Pax hominibus*, and he
alone says it because the *Gloria* was originally reserved to
bishops.

The word "collect" is said to be derived either from the
prayer *ad collectam*, that is, said over the assembled people,
or from the prayer said by the president of the assembly to
sum up and gather together (*colligere*) the intentions of the
faithful. This first prayer of the Mass is prefaced by the
priest's invitation to prayer (*Oremus*, "Let us pray"). At penitential seasons (and still nowadays on certain days of Lent,
Good Friday, the Easter Vigil, Ember days) the deacon then
gave the order to kneel—*flectamus genua*. In any case, after
Oremus the congregation remained for a moment or two in
silent prayer—a practice now happily restored on Good
Friday and Easter night. On occasion (Good Friday, for
example) a short invitatory indicated the intention for prayer
before the congregation knelt. The celebrant chants the collect
in the ancient attitude of the *Orantes*, standing and with arms
raised. According to tradition he is turned towards the east,
in the direction of the earthly paradise, of Calvary and, so it
was thought, of the *parousia* or Christ's return in glory, so
that the celebrant in those churches where the sanctuary is at
the east end is obliged to turn his back to the faithful.

Originally only one collect was said; subsequently they were
increased in number, probably to commemorate the minor
feasts superseded by more important festivals and also, perhaps, to take the place of the "prayer of the faithful" before
the offertory. The most recent rubrics have reduced the number of collects: there should never be more than three on
ordinary days or two on Sundays. At first the celebrant improvised the collect; the Missal subsequently preserved only
the most beautiful and the shortest. The most ancient collects
are those to be found in the Leonine sacramentary, but they
are of earlier date than this; it has been conjectured that

several of them are the work of St Damasus (366–84). These venerable forms of prayer thus bring us in contact with almost all generations of Christians.

The authentic tradition of the collect is to invoke God the Father by the mediation of his divine Son in the unity of the Holy Spirit. In private prayer there have always been forms addressed to the Son alone, but it was only about the year 1000, under anti-Arian Gallican influence, that collects began to be so addressed, thus modifying slightly the meaning of the ancient text (e.g. the collects of the Sundays of Advent). Collects are never addressed to the Holy Spirit and the three divine Persons are always mentioned in the conclusion. Of course, these prayers are made in the name of the Church and are in the plural.

Doctrinally, collects are of considerable interest and form a privileged element of the liturgy regarded as an expression of the faith of the Church and as a theological source. Among other points of dogma the perfections of God, the fall and redemption of man, the mysteries of Christ are all given expression in the collects; on those of the Sundays after Pentecost could be founded a short treatise on grace. They begin always with a solemn invocation—God, Lord, Almighty, everlasting God; then comes a reminder of a divine attribute, a mystery of faith or an example of a saint; lastly, there is a request, sometimes of a general nature, connected with what has preceded—God's help is asked for the various needs of a Christian: temporal requirements are not forgotten which is hardly surprising in view of the characteristic directness of the Romans. The collect is concluded by *Per Dominum* ("Through our Lord").

It has sometimes been said that the collects are not sufficiently inspired by the Bible and the Gospel, that they are wanting in emotion and display an almost stoical gravity. But it is impossible not to admire their succinctness, doctrinal value, harmonious elegance and symmetry of style. Their lyrical quality, which emerges on occasion, remains nevertheless unobtrusive and controlled, and it is probably well that it is so for a prayer made in the name of all should be sober, founded on unchangeable dogma and with a temperate appeal to the emotions.

The harmony of the Roman collects is derived principally from their rhythmic structure based on the quantity of the syllables, according to the rules laid down by Cicero and on the position of the accents at the end of a clause; sometimes, also, there is rhyme or assonance. There are four types of cadences in the Roman *cursus*; the three first are to be found in the well-known collect of the Angelus which may be used as an example.

1. The *cursus planus*: a word accentuated on the penultimate syllable is followed by a word of three syllables also accentuated on the penultimate syllable; that is, the accents are placed on the second and fifth syllables from the end:

méntibus nóstris infúnde.

2. The *cursus tardus*: a word accentuated on the penultimate syllable is followed by a word of four syllables accentuated on the ante-penultimate syllable, that is, accents on the third and sixth syllable from the end:.

Incarnatiónem cognóvimus.

3. *Cursus velox*, the most solemn and also the most elegant: a word of three syllables or more accentuated on the ante-penultimate is followed by a word of four syllables accentuated on the penultimate; that is, accents on the second and seventh syllable from the end:

Glóriam perducámur.
saécula saeculórum.

4. Lastly the di- or tri-spondiac *cursus*: three successive spondees or trochees; that is, accents on the second and sixth syllables from the end:

mórte reserásti (Easter)
illustratióne docúisti (Pentecost).

With few exceptions all the collects of the Leonine and Gelasian sacramentaries follow the rules of the *cursus*. And the same is true of the prefaces, certain patristic texts and many pontifical documents down to the Middle Ages, and even to our own days.

Readers unacquainted with Latin are asked to excuse these technical details which cannot be illustrated by translations. The preceding remarks on the *cursus* will be made clearer by the following examples taken from the finest of the collects. Those who know Latin will appreciate the original text, while the translation should reveal to all the dogmatic importance and spiritual value of the Roman collect.

Christmas (*midnight*)

Deus, qui hanc sacratissimam noctem veri luminis fecisti illustratione clarescere: da, quaesumus; ut cujus lucis mysteria in terra cognovimus, ejus quoque gaudiis in caelo perfruamur.

God, who hast made this most sacred night glow with the radiance of the true light, we pray thee grant that we may share to the full in heaven the joys of that Light whom we have known sacramentally on earth.

Christmas (*daybreak*)

Da nobis, quaesumus, omnipotens Deus: ut, qui nova incarnati Verbi tui luce perfundimur; hoc in nostro resplendeat opere, quod per fidem fulget in mente.

Grant, we pray thee, almighty God, that we who are bathed in the new light of thy incarnate Word may show forth in our deeds the light that by faith shines in our hearts.

Sunday in the Octave of Christmas

Omnipotens sempiterne Deus, dirige actus nostros in beneplacito tuo: ut in nomine dilecti Filii tui mereamur bonis operibus abundare.

Almighty, everlasting God, direct our actions according to thy pleasure. In the name of thy beloved Son let us be counted worthy to abound in good works.

Baptism of our Lord (January 13th)

Deus, cujus Unigenitus in substantia nostrae carnis apparuit: praesta, quaesumus; ut per eum, quem similem nobis foris agnovimus, intus reformari mereamur.

O God, whose only-begotten Son appeared in the substance of our flesh, grant us the grace to be inwardly refashioned by him who shared our outward likeness.

Palm Sunday

Deus, quem diligere et amare justitia est, ineffabilis gratiae tuae in nobis dona multiplica: et qui fecisti nos in morte Filii tui sperare quae credimus; fac nos eodem resurgente pervenire quo tendimus.

O God, whom to love with heart and mind is righteousness, multiply in us the gifts of thy transcendent grace; and since by thy Son's death thou hast given us hope of those things in which we believe, grant us by his resurrection to reach our journey's end.

Easter Sunday

(original text from the Gelasian sacramentary)

Deus qui hodierna die per Unigenitum tuum aeternitatis nobis aditum, devicta morte reserasti; da nobis quaesumus, ut qui resurrectionis Dominicae solemnia colimus, per innovationem tui Spiritus a morte animae resurgamus.

God, who on this day through thy only-begotten Son hast vanquished death and unlocked for us the gate of everlasting life; grant us, we pray, that as we celebrate the festival of our Lord's resurrection we may rise again from the death of our souls by the renewal of thy Spirit.

The collect in the present Missal is identical in the first part, but the second is very general in sense without specific reference to the feast.

Fourth Sunday after Easter

Deus, qui fidelium mentes unius efficis voluntatis: da populis tuis id amare quod praecipis, id desiderare quod promittis; ut inter mundanas varietates ibi nostra fixa sint corda, ubi vera sunt gaudia.

O God, by whose action the faithful are united in goodwill, incline thy people everywhere to love what thou commandest and to desire what thou dost promise, so that, among the changes of this world, our hearts may be set upon the one true home of joy.

Third Sunday after Pentecost

Protector in te sperantium, Deus, sine quo nihil est validum, nihil sanctum: multiplica super nos misericordiam tuam; ut, te rectore, te duce, sic transeamus per bona temporalia, ut non amittamus aeterna.

O God, protector of those who trust in thee, without whom nothing is strong, nothing is holy, increase thy mercy towards us, so that with thee for our ruler and guide, we may so pass through the good things of this world as not to lose those of the world to come.

SS. Peter and Paul (June 29th)

Deus, qui hodiernam diem Apostolorum tuorum Petri et Pauli martyrio consecrasti: da Ecclesiae tuae eorum in omnibus sequi praeceptum; per quos religionis sumpsit exordium.

O God, who hast made this day sacred by the martyrdom of thy apostles Peter and Paul, grant that thy Church may in all things follow the teaching of those from whom she received the first beginnings of the faith.

These short quotations, it is hoped, will arouse the desire to study and meditate on the collects which offer spiritual teaching of a high order throughout the year.

The finely phrased conclusion with which the collects end is worthy of special attention:

| Per Dominum nostrum Jesum Christum Filium tuum, qui tecum vivit et regnat in unitate Spiritus sancti, Deus, per omnia saecula saeculorum. | Through our Lord Jesus Christ, thy Son, who is God living and reigning with thee, in the unity of the Holy Spirit, for ever and ever. |

It appeals to Christ's merits and mediation, not only by asking him to intercede for us but by regarding him as the instrument of the Father's almighty power, and by associating him in the pouring out of grace. It is indeed the prayer in "his Name" that our Lord required of his apostles. "Whatever request you make of the Father in my name, I will grant" (John 14. 14). Our Lord is not only our intercessor; indivisibly with the Father he is the object of our prayer. By praying in this way and proclaiming his Godhead while imploring his mediation the Church interprets his intentions perfectly. The last words *in unitate Spiritus Sancti* are not absolutely clear: they can be seen as an act of faith in the divinity of the Holy Spirit and in the unity of the divine Persons, or they may be taken to refer to the unity established by the Holy Spirit, the unity of the Church filled with the Holy Spirit, an allusion to Eph. 4. 3. It is difficult to decide which is the true meaning.

As he concludes this formula the priest joins his hands and bows his head at the name of Jesus, a gesture of homage, inspired possibly by feudal law.

The recitative chant to which the collect is sung, especially if the older tone (*tonus antiquior*) is used, imparts a particularly natural and religious character to it, admirably completes the general impression and combining with the soberness of the words makes the collect a little masterpiece of dignity, grandeur, doctrine, piety and art. The collect indeed should be regarded as one of the principal prayers of the liturgy of the day, especially as it is repeated at the end of the hours of the Office which serve as a framework for the Mass. Particular attention should therefore be paid to it and it should form a fruitful subject for meditation.

In the Middle Ages the collect was sometimes followed by acclamations of praise (or *Laudes*) in honour of the pope, the sovereign or the bishop, with the majestic refrain *Christus vincit* and invocations to Christ and the saints for each intention as it was announced. These *Laudes* are still in use at the papal coronation Mass and in some cathedrals on important feast days.[1]

The collect concludes the first part of the fore-Mass. The prayers and chants have immersed the faithful in an atmosphere of repentance, praise and prayer which forms an excellent preparation for profitable hearing of the Word of God in the readings taken from the Old and New Testaments.

[1] They are sometimes termed Carolingian litanies or acclamations, probably on account of their introduction at the time of Charlemagne.

CHAPTER V

THE FORE-MASS:
THE LESSONS

THE EPISTLE

After the service of prayer comes the service of lessons; Christ is not only high priest but also teacher and prophet.

In the service of lessons we encounter once again the ancient Jewish usage. Every Sabbath day there was a meeting at the synagogue to hear reading of the Law and a commentary on it; the proceedings concluded with prayers and a blessing by a priest, if one was present.

The old Roman Mass contained three lessons—one from the Old Testament, one from the New and the last from the Gospel. This is still the case on the Wednesdays in Ember weeks, the Wednesday after Mid-Lent (*Laetare*) Sunday and on the Wednesday and Friday of Holy Week. The Ambrosian liturgy in use in Milan and the Dominican liturgy have also retained the three lessons on certain days. On the Saturdays of the Ember weeks and on Holy Saturday the Roman Mass contained twelve lessons, reduced to six by St Gregory the Great, except for Holy Saturday which until the recent reform retained the twelve lessons in addition to the Epistle of the Mass; these supplementary lessons did not belong to the Mass itself but formed part of the preparatory vigil. At the time of St Gregory there was only one Epistle at Mass taken from the Old or New Testament. The lessons were chanted at a raised ambo, the reader facing the people.

The few Masses nowadays with two Epistles take them both from the Old Testament. The first is chanted by a reader and the second by the subdeacon; as the Gospel is reserved to the deacon an ascending order of importance is thus suitably observed. The present rubrics take it for granted that the subdeacon turns his back on the congregation, a somewhat anomalous practice; the existence of an ambo in some churches and the tolerance of some bishops are both tending to modify this usage. The Epistle is sung to the right of the altar, that is, to the left of the bishop whose throne is taken as being at the centre of the apse; the Gospel is naturally sung on his right. The chant of the Epistle is very simple; it is sung either *recto tono*, except for the interrogatory sentences, or to a slightly more ornate tone with inflexions only in the middle or at the end of the sentences. At the end the response *Deo gratias* is made and the subdeacon kneels to receive the celebrant's blessing.

The sequence of lessons appears to have been fixed during the period from St Leo to St Gregory, that is, between 405 and 604. For Advent, Lent, Easter and Whitsun appropriate passages have been chosen. For the rest of the time the books from which the Epistle is taken are read straight through, the extract for one day following immediately upon that of the previous day, a practice known as *lectio continua*. The Catholic Epistles are read between Easter and Whitsun; from Whitsun to Advent the Catholic Epistles are concluded and St Paul is begun; from Epiphany to Lent St Paul is continued. During penitential seasons the Epistle is taken from the New Testament on Sundays but during the week the Old Testament is read. There are certain obscurities about the present system which derive probably from the fact that it is the result of the combination of two or more earlier schemes. For the feasts of saints the choice of passages is eclectic and well-adapted for its purpose. In ancient times the acts of the martyrs and the letters of foreign bishops were sometimes read. Considerable attention is naturally paid to St Paul. Some liturgists would like to see introduced a more rational system of lessons so that the finest extracts were all included while certain obscure or difficult passages were omitted. It is to be hoped that the definitive reform of the Missal will take this into account.

In connection with the lessons the vexed question of the use of the vernacular in worship is especially prominent for it is obvious that the Word of God is proclaimed to the people in order that they should understand it. Present legislation does however provide possibilities for a reasonable compromise. At a sung Mass the celebrant is not obliged to sing the Epistle, the rubrics take it for granted that he will merely read it and it would not appear to be forbidden for it to be read at the same time in the vernacular. The Gospel can be read in the vernacular immediately after it has been chanted by the deacon. Permission has recently been given in France for both Epistle and Gospel to be read in the vernacular, by the subdeacon and deacon respectively, immediately after their chanting in Latin. It is unlikely that the Church will abandon the use of a universal liturgical language which possesses incontestable advantages, but she might well make concessions in this matter of the lessons.

INTERVENING CHANTS: GRADUAL, ALLELUIA, SEQUENCE, TRACT

These chants form a natural pause between the lessons and furnish an element of variety; the synagogue practice of singing the psalms is well known. The gradual represents in fact the oldest and most solemn use of the Psalter at Mass. It is a psalm sung for its own sake whereas the psalms of the introit, offertory and communion are intended as the accompaniment of a procession. The term gradual is derived from the fact that it was sung at the ambo or on one of the steps (Latin *gradus*) leading to it. At the period when there were still three lessons it followed the first. After each verse a refrain or response (*responsum*) was repeated by the people, just as is done nowadays at the invitatory at Matins. The addition of the *Alleluia* when the lessons were reduced to two, together with the embellishments of the melody, have restricted the gradual to its refrain and a single verse of the psalm; it is still allowed to repeat the response after the verse, but that is scarcely ever done outside monastic choirs so that it is difficult to recognize the gradual as a responsorial chant.

The text is usually taken from the Psalter; occasionally it is a sentence from the Epistle (e.g. on the Epiphany and St John the Baptist); very rarely it is an ecclesiastical composition (*Benedicta es tu* in the Mass of the B.V.M.). The melody is very elaborate. The neums (from *pneuma*, breath) follow one after another on the same syllable. There is less variety than with the introits; certain melodies recur frequently, set to different words. Several of them are very fine indeed; it will suffice to mention *Qui sedes* of the third Sunday of Advent, *Christus factus* of Maundy Thursday, *Haec dies* of Easter, *Constitues* of SS. Peter and Paul and *Requiem* of the Mass of the dead. Certain penitential Sundays (Septuagesima, Quinquagesima, third Sunday of Lent, first Passion Sunday) have graduals of a curiously archaic character. The gradual, which is frequently of considerable musical difficulty, can only be carried out by a schola. For the faithful the gradual and *Alleluia* are meditative chants in which the teaching develops into prayer with the help of poetry and music. It is a pity that in order to gain a few minutes or to avoid the effort required to learn the chant the gradual and *Alleluia* are often monotoned, or else omitted altogether.

The *Alleluia* probably followed the second lesson when there were three; nowadays it is almost always joined to the gradual. Before St Gregory it comprised only the word *alleluia*, a Hebrew term meaning "praise Yahweh" followed by a long vocalization or *jubilus* on the last syllable this prolonged; it was a chant of joy in which the Christian was content to praise God without words. Subsequently a text was added and the responsorial form adopted with the repetition of the refrain *Alleluia* after the verse. Until the time of St

Gregory it was only sung at Eastertide; this pope extended its use to all the Sundays in the year outside Lent and its preparation (the three preceding Sundays); it is also sung on the feasts of saints at the same period of the year. Eastertide has even a double *Alleluia* with two verses, the first of which replaces the gradual. The text is usually taken from the Psalter, but on occasion it comes from the Epistle or Gospel (on the Epiphany, for example, Easter Sunday and Monday, and Corpus Christi, etc.). Not infrequently it is an ecclesiastical composition (fourth Sunday of Advent, third Mass of Christmas, Whitsunday, St Lawrence, the Assumption, St Martin, Mass of the B.V.M., etc.).

The *Alleluia* prepares us by an entirely interior joy for the good news of the Gospel. In the melody, which is more ornate than that of the gradual, Gregorian chant displays its resources to the full, and provided that the execution is good this chant produces a profound impression. There is a very large variety of melodies and those adapted to several different texts are few (first Sunday of Advent and Christmas midnight Mass— third Mass of Christmas, the feasts on the following days, Epiphany and St Peter—St Lawrence and Corpus Christi) and by far the greater number are sung only once a year. Many are real masterpieces; it will suffice to mention in this category *Veni Domine* of the fourth Sunday of Advent, *Dies sanctificatus* of Christmas, *Pascha nostrum* of Easter, *Emitte Spiritum* and *Veni Sancte* of Whitsun, *Caro mea* of Corpus Christi and *Venite ad me* of All Saints.

On certain occasions the *Alleluia* is continued by a sequence or continuation, a kind of prolongation of the words accompanying it. The sequences are of a more popular nature than the hymns of the Office; they are also called proses, from *prosa* or *prorsa, proversa oratio*, a style that goes straight on without taking account of the rules of metre. Sequences in the Middle Ages were very numerous indeed; the medieval English Missals for example, like those of France or Germany, contained a great number, several of them from the pen of

Adam of St Victor (who died in 1190). The Roman Missal
has kept only five which in their way are masterpieces:
Victimae paschali of Easter, full of restrained triumph; *Veni
Sancte Spiritus* of Whitsun, with a distinct mystical element
both in words and music; *Lauda Sion* of Corpus Christi,
solemn and doctrinal in tone; *Stabat Mater* for the two feasts
of our Lady's sorrows; *Dies Irae* for the dead, redolent of
great awe combined with confidence. The ideal is achieved
when the sequence is written in the same musical mode as the
Alleluia and thus constitutes a real sequence to it; this is the
case at Whitsun, Corpus Christi and with the *Stabat Mater*.
It is a pity that with the return to the Roman liturgy which
occurred from the time of the Missal of St Pius V onwards
and the disappearance of the local uses all over Europe so
many sequences were lost. A number of them were very
beautiful. Some, like the *Victimae Paschali*, contained the
germ of mystery plays from which the medieval theatre
developed. There were also sequences of a somewhat lighter
nature, that were sung at the banquet after the pope's, or
bishop's, solemn Mass.

From Septuagesima to Easter, and on certain days of a
penitential nature, the *Alleluia* is replaced by a psalm (or
tract), a fairly long continuation of the verses without an intervening refrain or response, which is sung straight through. In
reality it is probably the primitive psalm which has made
room for the *Alleluia*; at first it was responsorial in form.
Nowadays it is chanted antiphonally. The two musical modes
in which the tracts are written and the melodies which are
more austere than those of the graduals caused them to be
used exclusively during times of penance. Several of them are
made up of long series of verses (e.g. first Sunday of Lent,
Palm Sunday and Good Friday).

THE GOSPEL

The Gospel forms the culminating point of the fore-Mass
and the liturgy surrounds it with special marks of respect.

It will be remembered that in Ordo I the book of the Gospels is carried at the head of the entrance procession; as the Missal is placed on the altar only at the beginning of Mass it is only during the intervening chants that the deacon places the book of the Gospels there: this rite emphasizes the union between the Incarnate Word, symbolized by the altar, and the Word written in the Gospel. The deacon kneels down and recites *Munda cor*, asking God to purify his heart and lips as formerly he did for the prophet Isaias with a burning coal when entrusting him with his mission.[1] The deacon then asks the priest for a special blessing and a procession sets out for the place where the Gospel is chanted. At its head is borne the incense, the two acolytes with their candles follow, then the subdeacon and lastly the deacon, bearing reverently the book of the Gospels which should be as richly embellished as possible, following the example of the magnificently illuminated and bound manuscripts which have come down to us from the early Middle Ages and particularly the Carolingian period. In many cathedrals, out of respect for Christ present in a certain manner in his Word, all stand as the procession passes.

In churches facing east the Gospel was sung originally at the ambo on the north side, the deacon facing the men who were placed on the south side. Since the eleventh century—with the exception of local variations—he turns towards the north and this action is imitated by the celebrant of low Masses who goes from one side of the altar to the other (hence the familiar terms Epistle side and Gospel side) and turns slightly outwards to read the Gospel. The deacon, consequently, is on the bishop's right hand when the latter's throne is in the apse. The Middle Ages, greatly enamoured of allegorical explanations, considered that the Gospel should be sung towards the north, a region of cold and unhappiness whence came the barbarian invasions and where dwelt the devils whose influence it was necessary to combat. All stood

---

[1] Isaias 6. 6–7.

up straight and no longer leant on their staves save the bishop who continued (as he still does) to use his crozier for the purpose.

The deacon sings *Dominus vobiscum* and then announces the Gospel from which the day's extract is taken. At the same time he makes the sign of the cross on the book and also on himself (on forehead, lips and breast); all present sign themselves in the same manner, a gesture signifying that we should profess our faith with mind and mouth and keep it ever intact in our hearts. Then the deacon incenses the book while those present answer, *Gloria tibi, Domine* ("Glory be to thee, O Lord").

Then, while the subdeacon holds the book and all present in profound recollection listen to Christ, the deacon sings, "At that time, Jesus said to his disciples . . ." Three different tones for the Gospel are provided; that called the ancient tone (*tonus antiquior*) is especially pleasant. When the singing of the Gospel is over the subdeacon takes the open book to the celebrant who kisses the text saying, "By the words of the Gospel may our sins be blotted out". The acolytes say *Laus tibi Christe* ("Praise be to thee, O Christ") at the end of the Gospel. Until the thirteenth century the Gospel book was taken to all the clergy, and sometimes to all the faithful as well, for them to kiss it. Nowadays this honour is reserved to royal personages and ambassadors. It would not be unfitting for the congregation to kiss their own book at this moment.

It seems that until the fourth century at Rome the catechumens were dismissed before the Gospel which was solemnly "delivered" to them a few weeks before baptism, on the Wednesday after the fourth Sunday of Lent. The book of the Gospels is placed on the shoulders of new bishops during part of the ceremony of their consecration and the Church has preserved the custom of having the oaths which she requires on certain important occasions taken on the book of the Gospels.

The choice of passages has been made with great care for Advent, Christmas, the Sundays of Lent, Easter and Whitsun;

often during Lent and on feasts there is a connection between
the Epistle and Gospel; it also happens that the choice of
certain passages is governed by some feature concerning the
stational church or by the name of its titular.[1] Outside these
special periods the Gospels are read straight through, another
instance of the *lectio continua*. From the fourth Sunday of
Lent to Whitsun (except for Holy Week) the Gospel of St John
is read. From Whitsun to Advent and from the Epiphany to
the fourth Sunday of Lent passages are taken from the synoptic
Gospels. The feasts of saints are independent of the seasonal
cycle and have Gospels adapted to their purpose. The Gospel
usually provides the leading thought of the Mass of the day.
Although obviously the choice of extracts might be better
arranged and the absence of certain fine passages is to be
regretted, the lessons of the fore-Mass nevertheless furnish for
those who follow them regularly a spiritual education of great
value; they are a help in re-living each year the chief mysteries
of our redemption and they have led many souls to contact
with the Word of God, the more fruitful in that it has occurred
within the context of the Mass where it acquires a particular
efficacy.

THE HOMILY

The homily after the Gospel far from being an extra constitutes one of the oldest parts of the liturgy. It was in use in
the worship of the synagogue and our Saviour himself explained a passage from Isaias in the synagogue at Nazareth
(Luke 4. 16–22). In the early Church at Rome it was a somewhat rare occurrence, nevertheless we possess homilies by St
Leo and St Gregory; previously St Augustine preached a great
many in his church at Hippo. The repugnance for sermons
displayed by many of the faithful nowadays, to the point of

---

[1] Thus on the Saturday after the third Sunday of Lent the station is
at St Susanna and it is for this reason that the lesson from Daniel
(13. 1–62) with the story of another Susanna is read, and the Gospel
is that of the woman taken in adultery. [*Trans.*]

going to great lengths to discover a Mass without one, is due
no doubt to the general rush of modern life; also, it must be
recognized, the mediocrity of much preaching does not make
it attractive. The homily is a simple form of preaching, and
by no means a set or formal speech; traditionally it consists
in a commentary on one of the lessons of the Mass; if it is prepared and given with pastoral concern for the needs of the
faithful it is very fruitful and causes boredom to no one,
especially if it is short. The instruction of the faithful and
preaching of the Word of God are essential duties of parish
priests; in the atmosphere with which preaching is surrounded
at Mass it should touch the hearts of the congregation and
so gradually form earnest Christians.

Nowadays, in some countries, certain prayers are said
before the sermon at Mass[1]; this is the exact opposite of
ancient custom. These prayers no doubt take the place of the
"prayer of the faithful" which has disappeared from the offertory[2] and the list of the dead (anniversaries etc.) read out at
this point is possibly a relic of the diptychs. The general absolution and plenary indulgence granted on certain feast days
would be better at this place than at the end of Mass; this
was the custom in the Middle Ages when possibly this rite
took the place of the dismissal of the catechumens and public
penitents which had fallen into disuse.

THE CREDO

The creed is the answer to the Gospel and the climax of
the fore-Mass; when necessary it takes the place of the sermon
and forms a direct introduction to the holy sacrifice. It can
be regarded as a reminder of the recitation of the creed by the
catechumens immediately before baptism.

Our creed was not drawn up for use at Mass; it is a
rearrangement of the baptismal creed of Jerusalem in the
fourth century. It is called the Nicene-Constantinopolitan

[1] Like the "Bidding prayers" in medieval England, for example, and
still in some dioceses in France the prayers of the *prône*. [*Trans.*]

[2] See Jungmann, *op. cit.*, I, pp. 480–90.

Creed because it is a summary of the faith proclaimed in the two councils of this name (Nicea 325, Constantinople 391). At Nicea only a shorter form was drafted and Constantinople formulated no creed. It was the Council of Chalcedon in 451 which really established this fine profession of faith which had been drawn up in the intervening years.

The creed was first inserted in the Mass in the Eastern liturgies. In 589 the Spanish Visigoths adopted it and recited it before the Lord's Prayer. Charlemagne ordered it to be said in its present position in the palatine chapel at Aachen as a protest against the errors of the Spanish bishops concerning the Incarnation. It was not adopted in Rome until 1014, and then only on Sundays and feasts that are more or less directly referred to in it. The genuflection at *Et incarnatus* originated in the eleventh century and the *Filioque* became obligatory at a relatively late date.[1] The sign of the cross is made at the end as in the *Gloria*; it is possibly a development from the gesture of touching the forehead at mention of the resurrection of the dead. The following is a translation of this ancient document. It is in the singular as is fitting in view of its origins in the baptismal liturgy.

I believe in one God, the almighty Father, maker of heaven and earth, and of all things visible and invisible.

And in one Lord Jesus Christ, the only-begotten Son of God, born of the Father before all ages; God from God, light from light, true God from true God; begotten, not made, of one essence with the Father; through whom all things were made.

He for us men, and for our salvation, came down from heaven, and was incarnate by the Holy Ghost from the virgin Mary; and was made man.

He was also crucified for our sake under Pontius Pilate: suffered and was buried. And the third day he rose again according to the Scriptures. And he ascended into heaven, and is seated at the right hand of the Father. He will come again with glory to judge the living and the dead; and of his reign there will be no end.

[1] See volumes 17 and 18 of this series.

I believe too in the Holy Spirit, Lord and life-giver, who proceeds from the Father and the Son; who together with the Father and the Son is adored and glorified; who spoke through the prophets.

And I believe in one holy, catholic and apostolic Church. I acknowledge one baptism for the remission of sins. And I look forward to the resurrection of the dead, and the life of the world to come. Amen.

The Vatican Gradual includes four plainchant settings of the creed; except for the third, which is more ornate and elegant, they are almost monosyllabic recitatives. The first, of admirable simplicity, is unobtrusively archaic; the fourth is vigorous and forceful, suitable for singing by a large congregation.

The creed is well placed at this point in the Mass as a profession of the faith which has already been proclaimed in the chants and lessons; it takes on a character of pride in, and glad adherence to, the Christian message and thus forms an excellent introduction to the offering of the sacrifice. Until recent years it occurred fairly frequently at Mass; the latest reform reserves its use to days of a certain solemnity, that is, to Sundays and the most important feast days.

CHAPTER VI

PREPARATION OF THE MYSTERY: THE OFFERTORY

THE OFFERING OF BREAD AND WINE

With the offertory begins the Mass properly so called, from
which the catechumens were excluded, and the oblation of the
holy sacrifice. The initial *Oremus* is followed by no prayer;
it is the last remaining trace of the *prayer of the faithful* in
which were set before God the various needs of the Church;
the solemn collects on Good Friday give an idea of the form
it took. Some liturgists would like to see it restored on the
most important days when it would suitably emphasize the
universal nature of the prayer of the Church although it is
true, of course, that (in some places) the prayers before the
sermon, and the intercessory prayers of the canon to some
extent take its place. The prayer of the faithful, in addition
to its intrinsic character, was also the expression of an extremely ancient tradition; St Justin bears witness to its
existence in the second century. Nevertheless, it disappeared
at an early date; it is found for the last time in Ordo I as the
conclusion of a separate office of lessons on the morning of
Wednesday in Holy Week.

The Gelasian sacramentary at this point gives two collects,
one of which is the secret or prayer over the offerings. The
other, which has completely disappeared, is probably the
equivalent of the prayer *super sindonem* of the Ambrosian

rite, that is, the prayer said at the spreading of the altar cloth. Mentally, and in spite of the interval between the two, we can connect the present *Oremus* with the secret, for it was formerly said aloud like the collect. In those early days there was no other offertory prayer.

At the end of the second century, as may be seen from St Irenaeus and Tertullian, there was a direct connection between the voluntary contributions of the faithful and the Eucharist; in the fourth century almost everywhere, though not invariably, an offering of bread and wine made by them is to be found at this point in the liturgy. As described in a previous chapter, the offertory occasioned a procession which, at the time of St Augustine, was accompanied by a chant composed, as at the introit, of a refrain or antiphon interspersed between several verses of a psalm; the antiphon itself was often taken from the psalter. The gradual disappearance of the offertory procession after the ninth and tenth centuries led to the suppression of the psalm; the antiphon alone has been preserved. There is still a refrain in Masses of the Dead (and see also the offertory of the twenty-third Sunday after Pentecost) at which, in fact, in many places the offering by the congregation at this point has been retained though it is no longer bread and wine that is offered but an alms in the form of money. The antiphon has become an extremely ornate chant; with its mystical, and on occasion joyful, character it forms an apt expression of the spontaneity of offering and is an invitation to recollection. This may be seen clearly by perusal of some of the offertories like those for the Epiphany, the second Sunday in Lent, Palm Sunday, Easter Monday, the fourth Sunday after Easter, Whit Sunday and the Mass for the dedication of a church.

The loaves offered were household bread, but specially prepared, round and marked with a cross or else in the shape of a crown. In about the ninth century, a stricter view of the care required in providing the matter of the sacrifice became prevalent; it was to be as beautiful and pure as possible. The

use of unleavened bread shaped like a coin became common
and finally obligatory in the west. It had the advantage of
more accurately recalling the institution since our Saviour
celebrated the Last Supper with the unleavened bread of the
Passover meal, but it obviously contributed to the disappearance of the offering by the faithful and of the fraction.
The altar breads used frequently to be arranged in somewhat
complicated patterns on the altar and a symbolic meaning was
attached to the practice which is still observed in the Byzantine liturgy. The wine was sometimes red wine, which was
appropriate and remains lawful, but has the disadvantage of
staining the altar linen. Often money was brought at the offertory and even deeds of gift in favour of churches. These gifts,
with no direct connection with the sacrifice, were soon dis-
sociated from the offering of bread and wine and the celebrant
ceased to receive them in person; they are at the origin of the
collections at, and the stipends for, Mass. When the offering by
the faithful was over the bread and wine necessary for the
communion were placed on the altar; sometimes a considerable quantity was required as is shown by, among others, the
secret for St John the Baptist—"we heap up (*cumulamus*)
gifts upon the altar". What was not required for consecration
was used for the support of the clergy and the poor. A portion
could be given to those who did not communicate and this is
the origin of the blessed bread (*pain bénit*) distributed in some
countries; as a consequence its blessing had to take place at
the offertory.

Offering in the sense described above is no longer in use
save at ordinations (the ordinands each bring a candle), at the
consecration of bishops (candles, bread and wine) and, at
Rome, in canonization Masses. At an early date the non-
Roman rites adopted the custom of preparing the gifts before
the beginning of the liturgy and of having them brought in
solemn procession at the appropriate time, but by the clergy
alone; this is still the practice in the Byzantine liturgy and in
certain cathedrals in Europe. The Dominicans, Calced Car-

melites and Carthusians prepare the chalice before beginning Mass and, at a sung Mass, during the gradual.

The offering by the people had the advantage of bringing out clearly the idea that the sacrifice is not offered by the priest alone but also by all those present; the faithful, by virtue of their baptism, are invested with a "royal priesthood" (1 Peter 2. 9), secondary and subordinate but none the less real. In our own day more or less successful attempts have been made to revive the offertory procession. The faithful are asked themselves to place in a ciborium altar breads from a basket at the entrance to the church; but these altar breads have not been prepared by them and the rite thus loses part of its meaning. Would it not be better to endow the collection with a more spiritual meaning? In some churches, the whole collection, which has been made as unobtrusively as possible, is carried near to the altar by servers and held aloft by them while the celebrant says the secret; in this way is emphasized in a suitable manner the union of the holy sacrifice with freely given alms. Sometimes gifts in kind are brought at the offertory; at least their owners should really *give* them, for there seems no sense in the "offering", for example, of tools for work which their owners take back afterwards; it would be more suitable to have them blessed after Mass with one of the formulas provided by the Ritual for this purpose; in this way the intention of sanctifying daily work would be shown with sufficient clarity.

The rites and prayers of the oblation of the bread and wine were amplified considerably in the Middle Ages; St Pius V's Missal retained a part of them and it will be fitting at this point to explain them.

The deacon unfolds the corporal during the *Credo*, or if it is not said, after the *Oremus*. The subdeacon brings the chalice with the humeral veil (of which the chalice veil is a reduced form) because at the time when communion was given under both kinds the chalice was very heavy and the veil, worn round the neck, took part of the weight; he retains this veil until the *Pater noster* in order to hold the paten which originally was a plate of some size and was removed from the altar because it was cumbersome.

The deacon presents the paten and hosts to the priest who offers them, saying the prayer *Suspice sancte Pater*; he asks God to receive them for the pardon of his sins, for the faithful who are present and for all Christians, living or dead. The prayer is in the singular and therefore of relatively recent introduction.

Meanwhile the deacon and subdeacon put wine and a drop of water into the chalice. This admixture is in accordance with the custom of ancient peoples and of the passover rite observed by our Lord at the Last Supper. Its use in the liturgy is mentioned by St Irenaeus (second century) and its symbolism is explained by St Cyprian: it signifies the union of Christ and the Church and the unity of Christian people, a point that is well brought out by the prayer recited by the priest.[1]

It is a collect originally composed for Christmas adapted to its present purpose by a short addition: "O God, by whom the dignity of human nature was wondrously established and yet more wondrously restored, grant that through the sacramental rite of this water and wine we may have fellowship in the Godhead of him who deigned to share our manhood, Jesus Christ, thy Son, our Lord."

The Church regards this rite as of great importance and insists upon its observance; at the same time the priest makes a sign of the cross to bless the water which represents the faithful; he omits it only at Masses for the dead when attention is concentrated on the souls of the departed. Cardinal Mercier's discerning lines fall naturally into place here:

---

[1] Other liturgies (e.g. Lyon, Carthusians) see in the mixing of water with the wine a symbol of the blood and water which flowed from the side of our crucified Saviour, and this is expressed in the prayer recited at the ceremony of admixture: *De latere Domini nostri Jesu Christi exivit sanguis et aqua*: "From the side of our Lord Jesus Christ came forth blood and water...." [*Trans.*]

I am the little drop of water absorbed by the wine of the Mass;
And the wine of the Mass becomes the blood of the Man-God;
And the Man-God is substantially one with the Holy Trinity;
The little drop of water is carried away in the river of life of
      the Holy Trinity;
Will this little drop of water, destined to play a part in the
      sacrifice of the Mass, ever be clear and pure enough?

Next the deacon presents the chalice to the priest and both together recite the prayer *Offerimus* of the offering of the wine, asking that it may ascend with a sweet fragrance in the presence of God's majesty for the salvation of the whole world. As we know, the chalice was the special province of the deacon; he used to help the priest to raise it up by holding it by the handles with which it was furnished. The priest adds a prayer of repentance and humility, *In spiritu humilitatis*, which states that both he and the faithful ask that their sacrifice may be pleasing to God. There follows a short invocation, *Veni sanctificator,* in which the Middle Ages saw an invocation of the Holy Spirit, making it thus a sort of *epiclesis*, asking for his coming down over the gifts in order to transform them; but this meaning is by no means certain as the formula is not explicit. During these prayers the subdeacon enfolds the paten in his veil and goes down to the foot of the altar. At low Mass the priest leaves the paten on the altar, but covers it with the corporal and the purificator.

The offertory thus accomplished forms as it were a first sanctification of the bread and wine which it withdraws from ordinary use. Other rites and formulas now complete it.

THE INCENSING, LAVABO AND SECRET

The incensing which takes place at this point is of Carolingian origin; it was only introduced in Rome in the twelfth century, and its ceremonial was definitively fixed a little later. The celebrant places incense in the thurible, asking God to bless it; at the same time he calls on the intercession of St

Michael, probably identified with the angel in the Apocalypse
(8. 3) who offers to God the prayers of the saints.[1]

The priest incenses the hosts and chalice in the form of a
cross and circlewise and then the crucifix and altar. Next, the
deacon incenses the celebrant and the choir and is himself
incensed by the thurifer who, finally, incenses the congregation. Down the ages this rite has been the cause of not a few
disputes concerning order of precedence which nonetheless
impair not at all its lofty significance. The incensing of the
oblation and the altar symbolizes the prayers of the Church
rising up to God like a cloud of incense, as is shown by the
verses of the psalm said at the time (Psalm 140. 2–4); it is an
expression, therefore, of the sanctification of the objects that
it affects. The incensing of persons signifies their participation
in the offering of these prayers and in the fire of divine love,
well symbolized by the burning of incense; it is also a mark
of honour as it is in the case of the crucifix. The incensing of
the Blessed Sacrament at exposition and Benediction has the
same meaning.

The *Lavabo*, in addition to its symbolic meaning (the only
one remaining at Masses without incense), is easily understood at this point (in former times after the handling of the
offerings) since its purpose is to cleanse the priest's hands. It
is accompanied by the recitation of a portion of a psalm
chosen on account of the first phrase, "With the pure in heart
I will wash my hands clean, and take my place among them
at thy altar, Lord" (Psalm 25. 6–12).

The celebrant then returns to the middle of the altar and
says the prayer *Suscipe Sancta Trinitas*, a prayer of offering
which is a summary of those that have gone before. It is of
Gallican origin but may well contain some ancient elements.

---

[1] It has often been pointed out that the angel "who stands at the
right hand of the altar of incense" is St Gabriel (Luke 1. 11, 18) and
most medieval Missals mentioned him by name. But no name is given
in the Apocalypse and it is possible that Michael was deliberately inserted into the Roman Missal as the defender of the Church and in
allusion to this verse. [*Trans.*]

It states that the offering is addressed to the Holy Trinity in memory of the mysteries of redemption—passion, resurrection and ascension—an important idea which recurs after the consecration. The sacrifice is also offered, it adds, in honour of the saints, especially of the Blessed Virgin Mary, St John the Baptist, SS. Peter and Paul and those whose relics are enclosed in the altar. This forms, as it were, a summary repetition of the offering previously made separately for the bread and wine, an offering which includes also the spiritual offering of the whole Church whose members present have testified that they offer themselves by participation in the gift of bread and wine which will represent them and be transformed into the divine Victim.

The offertory concludes with the *Orate fratres* and the secret. Turning to the people the priest, taking leave of them, so to speak, before entering on the solemn part of the liturgical action, asks their prayers: "Pray, brethren, that my sacrifice and yours may prove acceptable in the eyes of God the almighty Father." The answer to this request states some of the ends of sacrifice: it is a prayer that God may receive it at the hands of the priest "to the praise and glory of his name, for our welfare also and that of all his holy Church".

For the last time the secret then presents to God the gifts placed upon the altar. In fact it is the real, and formerly the only, prayer of offering, the *oratio super oblata* which concludes the offertory as the collect concludes the prayers at the entrance. It is in the same style and of the same period as the collect. The custom of saying it in a low voice originated in Gaul and it is from this, no doubt, that the name is derived, although various etymological explanations have been put forward, among others that of the prayer over the offerings "set apart", by deriving *secreta* from the verb *secernere* (to separate, set apart). The Roman secrets always allude to the offerings and ask in return for a grace in connection with the mystery celebrated on a particular day or merely with the bread and wine which are to be changed into the body and blood of Christ. Some of them are couched in terms which seem to mean that the consecration has already been effected and as if we had already received the body of Christ; the rites of the Mass constitute a single whole and the Christians of antiquity did not speculate on the precise moment at which consecration occurred. The body and blood of Christ are offered in advance, and in advance acquiescence in this oblation is expressed, just as the request for an ordination or the charter of a monastic profession is written beforehand. The Byzantine liturgy at the offertory procession pays to the bread and wine the same marks of respect that we do to the Blessed Sacrament. Other secrets cause us to offer our prayers, our penances, our whole selves. The following examples, translated into English, display that sober, austere and pervasive charm already encountered in the collects, more strongly marked by emphasis on the idea of offering though expressed less aptly and more succinctly.

First Sunday of Advent

Lord, may these dedicated offerings cleanse us by their mighty power and bring us all the purer to him who created them.

Second Sunday in Advent

Let our humble prayers and offerings move thy compassion, Lord. Since we can plead no merits of our own, let thy protection help us.

Third Sunday in Advent

May our dedicated offering, Lord, be sacrificed unceasingly to thee, so that the end for which thou didst ordain this holy rite may be fulfilled, and the miracle of thy saving work be wrought within us.

Ember Wednesday of Advent

May our fasting be acceptable to thee, Lord; may it atone for our sins, make us worthy of thy grace, and bring us the fulfilment of thy eternal promises.

Christmas: Midnight Mass

Accept, Lord, this day's festal offering, and in thy gracious bounty grant that through this interchange of sacred gifts, we may grow to be like him in whom our human nature is made one with thine.

Epiphany

Look favourably, Lord, upon thy Church's gifts. It is not gold that we offer now, nor frankincense and myrrh, but he who is proclaimed thereby, our sacrifice and our food, Jesus Christ, our Lord.

Ash Wednesday

Lord, make us truly fit to offer up these gifts, with which we celebrate the beginning of this sacred observance [that is, the mystery of Lent which will make us participate more fully in the redemption].

Thursday in Passion Week

O Lord our God, who hast commanded and prepared that these material things, created by thee for the support of our frail nature, should also be dedicated as offerings to thy name, grant that they may not only help us in this present life, but prove a pledge of immortality.

Maundy Thursday

We pray thee, holy Lord, almighty Father, eternal God, that Jesus Christ, thy Son, our Lord, who founded this day's eucharistic rite and bade his disciples perform it in memory of him, may himself make our offering acceptable to thee.

Easter Sunday

Accept, we pray thee, Lord, thy people's prayers and sacrificial gifts; and let the work begun here in our Easter rites bring us eternal healing at thy hand.

Whit Sunday

Hallow our proferred gifts, we beg thee, Lord, and cleanse our hearts by the light of the Holy Spirit.

Corpus Christi

Lord, be gracious to thy Church, we pray thee, and grant her those gifts of unity and peace of which our offerings here are symbols.

Ninth Sunday after Pentecost

Grant, we pray thee, Lord, that we may worthily and often take part in these rites, for each and every offering of this memorial sacrifice carries on the work of our redemption.

Since the secrets are said in a low voice they are not preceded by *Oremus*; in any case, this has already been said at the beginning of the offertory. The celebrant terminates the last of the secrets aloud, *Per omnia saecula saeculorum*, "For ever and ever," merely to indicate that he has concluded them and that the canon is about to begin.

*   *   *

Viewed as a whole the offertory appears somewhat complicated: the bread is offered, water is mixed with the wine, the wine is offered, the offerings are incensed; they are offered anew by the *Suscipe Sancta Trinitas* and a third time in saying the secret. All these prayers are an anticipation of the themes of the canon, a "little canon" as it was called in the Middle Ages. Possibly the coming reform of the Missal may effect some simplification here and restore to its proper prominence the venerable secret prayer.

It is fitting to observe at this point how greatly the offertory emphasizes the participation of the faithful in the sacrifice: it is offered by all and for all and it is also the offering of all. It is the more pleasing to God and fruitful for the Church to the degree that she is the holier and that each of her members strives to offer himself with Christ. Every offering made to God implies, in effect, the offering of ourselves; this is one of the aspects of every sacrificial action. From the earliest times the Fathers interpreted in this sense the addition of the drop of water to the chalice. "Because Christ bore us all in himself," says St Cyprian, "he who bore even our sins, we see signified in the water all peoples, and in the wine the blood of Christ. When the water is mixed with wine in the chalice, the people is joined to Christ. . . . If only the wine were offered the blood of Christ would be made present without us, if only the water, the people without Christ."[1]

For some years past this aspect of the Mass has been emphasized, either by trying to reintroduce the offering by the faithful, or by emphasizing the symbolism of the drop of water. It is a praiseworthy intention for it is important to convince the faithful that they should not be passive spectators and that their sacrifice should be united to Christ's. But it is no less important to avoid placing our own offering in the forefront for this would amount to a distortion of the meaning of the Mass.

It must not be forgotten indeed that, in accordance with the evidence of the most ancient liturgical texts, the only offering is that of the body and blood of Christ. The offering of the oblation (the bread and wine, gifts in kind, money) and even that of the faithful themselves in person derives all its value from union with the divine Victim. Our Lord is the only victim in the strict sense of the word; he alone sacrificed himself on the cross and thus obtained for us the remission of our sins. In like manner, he alone is offered on the altar and we can only offer him; it would be blasphemous to claim to offer ourselves with him in a strictly sacrificial sense. Nevertheless, we are closely bound up with, are inseparable from, him since we are members of his body. He offered us with himself on Calvary; with him and through him, the whole Church was henceforth united with his sacrifice. The fact that he is offered by her and for her at the altar requires that we should offer ourselves with Christ by an inward gift of self to God, in a life lived in a state of grace by fleeing from sin and by the crucifixion of evil propensities, in other terms in the state of victim in the moral sense of the word. This attitude of generosity in the love of God before all else and fidelity to duty, even to that of the most irksome kind, should be an enduring disposition; but there is no better time than at Mass to renew it and intensify it by offering our whole life and our

[1] *Letter* 63. 13.

whole being. It is in this derivative sense that the Church can be said to be a victim with Christ; she offers herself whole and entire on the altar and offers each of her members, even the indifferent ones. But this offering adds nothing to the atoning and propitiatory value of Christ's offering; there is an infinite distance between us and him and yet so closely are we united with him that he deigns to associate us with himself.[1]

[1] See A. M. Roguet, O.P., *Holy Mass, Approaches to the Mystery* (London, 1953). On this point, and on the theology of the Mass, see Volume 52 of the present series.

CHAPTER VII

THE CENTRAL ACT OF THE MYSTERY: THE EUCHARISTIC PRAYER AND CONSECRATION

GENERAL FEATURES OF THE CANON

Since the time of the ancient sacramentaries the term *canon* or *canon actionis* has been applied to this principal and almost invariable part of the Mass; its essential element is the narration of the Last Supper and it concludes with the doxology preceding the Lord's Prayer. From the anaphora of the *Apostolic Tradition* (quoted above) and other ancient texts it emerges clearly that the primitive form of the canon was a Preface (or formula of thanksgiving) sung straight through from the dialogue at the beginning until the final doxology, and not unlike the preface form still in use on Easter night for the *Exsultet* and the blessing of the baptismal water and that for the ordination of deacons and priests.

At an early date the unity of the anaphora was impaired by the introduction of the *Sanctus* (some liturgies inserted a formula beginning *Vere sanctus* in order to connect *Sanctus* and canon), and then by the addition of secondary elements, especially the Memento of the living and of the dead. The Roman canon, which rapidly found its way into all, and in other respects very different, western liturgies, goes back at least to the period of St Leo the Great (440–61) and possibly to that of St Damasus (366–84). Its unknown author certainly succeeded in composing a solemn prayer of great nobility which is emphasized by certain literary peculiarities—the parallelism, the construction of sentences, the use of twofold in threefold and sometimes fivefold terms in a balance that is always harmonious—so that it is impossible to read it in Latin without appreciating its beauty.

Additions have been made to the primitive kernel so that in the formation of the present canon several layers can be distinguished. The following, according to Mgr Batiffol[1] (though possibly he is a little too categorical), are the dates to be assigned to the various prayers:

Primitive period: Narration of the Last Supper: *Qui pridie.*

Period of St Leo or St Damasus: prayers vouched for by the *De Sacramentis* of St Ambrose but in a less polished and less complete form than in the present text:

> *Quam oblationem.*
> *Unde et memores.*
> *Supra quae propitio.*
> *Supplices te rogamus.*

Prayers whose existence is assumed in a letter from Innocent I (to Decentius, bishop of Gubbio, March 19th, 416):

> *Te igitur.*
> *Memento* of the living.

From the period of Symmachus (498–514) or Vigilius (c. 538, probably a little earlier, according to Jungmann)[2]:

> *Communicantes.*
> *Hanc igitur.*
> *Nobis quoque.*

Lastly, in the seventh century at the latest:

> *Memento* of the dead.

[1] P. Batiffol, *Leçons sur la messe*, Paris, 1919.
[2] Jungmann, *op. cit.*, I, p. 55 seq.

(The conclusion *Per Christum* of these prayers breaks the unity of the anaphora and emphasizes the lateness of their origin.)

Jungmann considers that the hand of St Leo can be discerned in several places and that the definitive form of the canon may well go back to Gelasius (492–6), but this is only a hypothesis. The most ancient manuscripts (seventh–eighth centuries) contain the present text with certain variations of detail. Consequently, we say these venerable prayers in union with the Christians of several centuries. They merit a detailed study which, while not clarifying all the obscure points, will help us to understand their meaning and to recite them with the reverence required by the sacrifice of the altar. Moreover, without undue subtlety a certain order can be discerned in the formulas added to the primitive anaphora: these are the prayers of intercession which, so to say, gather the whole Church together round the crucified and risen Christ—the Church militant and the faithful present, at the *Te igitur* and the *Memento* of the living; the Church triumphant of the saints, at the *Communicantes*; the Church suffering of the dead, at the second *Memento*; finally, in a special way, the priest and his assistants at the altar at the *Nobis quoque peccatoribus*. The universal nature of redemption is thus emphasized at the same time as its fruits are bestowed on all. As on the cross Christ draws all men to himself.[1]

For long the canon was said aloud, probably to a recitative, but simpler, tone like the preface. Recitation in a low voice appears towards the middle of the eighth century, and in the ninth century with Ordo Romanus II silent recitation became obligatory. In the east the practice was adopted much earlier. Everywhere the tendency was to surround the canon with respect and a sense of mystery and to reserve it to the celebrant alone.[2]

[1] John 12. 32.

[2] In the oriental liturgies the impression of mystery is enhanced by the iconostasis, a screen to which icons are attached, and by the curtain which hides the altar during the anaphora.

PREFACE AND SANCTUS

The name of preface is given to the variable part of the eucharistic prayer which occurs before the *Sanctus*. The term would be more accurate if it were confined to the preceding dialogue whose extreme antiquity has been shown to us by the anaphora of St Hippolytus. At an early date the word came to mean a solemn prayer said in the presence of the congregation and thus included the whole canon until it assumed the restricted sense given to it nowadays. Other liturgies use different terms—*illatio*, in the sense of oblation; *immolatio*, prayer during which the sacrifice is accomplished; *contestatio*, with the fine meaning of supreme witness to the faith.

While the canon became fixed in form the prefaces on the contrary varied according to the festivals celebrated. The Leonine sacramentary includes 267 of them, one for each Mass, the later Gelasian sacramentary 186; there are already far fewer in the Gregorian. St Pius V's Missal retained a very small number though this has been slightly increased since his day. The proliferation of early days certainly included much that was mediocre—on occasion an unexpected polemical note is struck or we find long exhortations unconnected with the fundamental theme. But it is a pity that almost all was sacrificed for very much of great value was laid aside. There is no reason why a reform of the Missal should not bring back into use many fine prefaces which have now been long forgotten. In the Greek liturgy the preface is invariable.

The principal theme finds expression in the *Gratias agamus* of the preliminary dialogue and in the first words of the preface itself, *Vere dignum*: it is a solemn tribute of adoration and thanksgiving offered to God for all his benefits, more especially for the coming of our Saviour and the redemption wrought by him. Adoration and thanksgiving are indeed the appropriate sentiments.

In the other prefaces three sections can be clearly discerned:

the introduction *Vere dignum* which is an expression of the supreme appropriateness and the duty of thanking God the Father almighty, the embolism or continuation which sets out the principal reasons for thanksgiving, often one of the mysteries of the life of our Lord—it always mentions in conclusion that the thanksgiving is made in his name—and this invocation of his mediation introduces a last section in which the celebrant recalls that the angels (the imposing enumeration of their orders, taken from Scripture, varies with the preface) adore God likewise through Jesus Christ[1] and calls on the faithful to unite with them by joining in the *Sanctus* which they ceaselessly repeat in the presence of the adorable Trinity. The following is the translation of the common preface in which the embolism is reduced to the words *Per Christum Dominum nostrum*:

Right indeed it is and just, proper and for our welfare, that we should always and everywhere give thanks to thee, holy Lord, almighty Father, eternal God, through Christ our Lord.

It is through him that thy majesty is praised by Angels, adored by Dominations, feared by Powers; through him that the heavens and the celestial Virtues join with the blessed Seraphim in one glad hymn of praise. We pray thee let our voices blend with theirs as we humbly praise thee, singing: *Sanctus* . . .

At Christmas the following embolism is said:

For through the mystery of the Word made flesh thy splendour has shone before our mind's eye with a new radiance, and through him whom we recognize as God made visible we are carried away in love of things invisible. Therefore it is with Angels and Archangels. . . .

At Passiontide:

By thy ordinance the salvation of mankind was accomplished on the wood of the cross, so that life might rise again there where death had its beginning, and that he who conquered through a tree should on a tree himself be conquered; through Christ our Lord.

[1] Colos. 2. 10: Christ is the head over all the angels.

At Easter:

Right indeed it is and just, proper and for our welfare to praise thee, Lord, at all times, but more triumphantly than ever on this day, when Christ our Passover was sacrificed. For he is the true Lamb who has taken away the sins of the world: he who by dying has brought our death to naught, and by rising again has restored us to life.

At the Ascension:

Through Christ our Lord who after his resurrection appeared openly to all his disciples and was lifted up to heaven before their eyes, so that he might grant us fellowship with his Godhead.

In spite of the obvious imperfection of any translation the vigour, the harmonious and succinct nature of these prefaces can be appreciated; they are models of the Roman liturgical style. They are sung by the celebrant to a simple, purely syllabic, recitative chant on ferial days and at Masses for the dead; on Sundays and feasts of saints the melody, slightly more ornate, brings out admirably the rhythm of the Latin phrase. For important festivals a special tone is provided for optional use; its additional long neums produce an imposing effect but possibly impair the beautiful simplicity of the ordinary festal preface. The priest has his arms outstretched as at the collect. This is the usual ancient attitude for prayer, and he retains it all through the canon except when he has to handle the host or chalice or make the signs of blessing.

Reference to the angels at the end of the preface serves as an introduction for the *Sanctus*. The first part is taken from the well-known vision of Isaias (already alluded to in the *Munda cor* before the Gospel). The prophet's actual words have been slightly modified and adapted. The *Benedictus* which follows repeats the acclamation of the crowd on Palm Sunday quoted by St Matthew (21. 9) which is already to be found, except for *Hosanna* in Ps. 117. 26. It is a heartfelt exclamation proclaiming the greatness of God and Christ and an act of faith in the mysteries about to be accomplished.

"Blessed is he who is coming in the name of the Lord!" The priest bows down as he invokes the God of *Sabaoth*, the God of hosts, that is, of the whole host of heaven and all beings created by God, especially the heavenly bodies (Gen. 2. 1) and the bell is rung to announce the central part of the eucharistic action. This imposing chant is wholly fitted to produce a profound religious impression entirely appropriate to the context.

The *Sanctus* appears to break the unity of the primitive canon by causing the congregation to intervene during a solemn prayer reserved to the priest. St Justin does not allude to it and it is absent from the anaphora of St Hippolytus. On the other hand, some ancient texts seem to presuppose its use, as for example St Clement of Rome's *Letter to the Corinthians* (chapter 34) of the end of the first century; it is to be found in the *Apostolic Constitutions* and in the anaphora of Serapion, bishop of Thmuis in Egypt in the fourth century. The ancient catalogue of the early popes, known as the *Liber Pontificalis*, is probably right in attributing the introduction of the *Sanctus* into the Mass to Sixtus II (119–28). In the fourth century it seems to have become almost the universal practice and to have been adopted by all liturgies. The *Benedictus* is somewhat later; it does not occur in the *Te Deum* which is composed on the model of an anaphora and contains only the *Sanctus*.

The only *Sanctus* chant which corresponds musically with the preface is the very simple one appointed for the ferial days of Lent and used also at Masses of the dead. The Gradual contains as many chants for the *Sanctus* as there are for the Kyrie with melodies which are to be commended for their religious gravity and variety. Polyphonic Masses have added considerably to the musical solemnity of the *Sanctus*, though the gradual consequence has been the postponement of the *Benedictus* until after the consecration; this custom was finally enjoined in a decree of the S. Congregation of Rites, though an authoritative opinion from the same source has recently stated that the decree will no longer be enforced.

It will be noticed that so far the eucharistic prayer makes no mention of the Holy Spirit. In fact it follows the order of the divine Persons. The Holy Spirit is mentioned in the epiclesis (in those liturgies which contain one) and always in the final doxology of the canon.

TE IGITUR

After saying the *Sanctus* the priest raises his hands, then joins them on the altar bowing low meanwhile. This beautiful gesture is like a silent prayer introducing the *Te igitur*: it forms, so to say, the entrance to the holy of holies.

> And so, through Jesus Christ, thy Son, our Lord, we humbly pray and beseech thee, most gracious Father, to accept and bless these offerings, these oblations, these holy unblemished sacrificial gifts, which we offer thee in the first place for thy holy Catholic Church, praying that thou wilt be pleased to keep and guide her in peace and unity throughout the world; together with thy servant our Pope N., and N., our bishop, and all who, faithful to true doctrine, are the guardians of the Catholic and apostolic faith.

Our Missals make the canon begin at this point. The initial T of the first word (*Te*) at an early date was made into the form of a cross and enriched with sumptuous illumination; in the Middle Ages the priest kissed this cross. Nowadays he kisses the altar. This very natural gesture emphasizes the intensity of the prayer already suggested by the profound bow at the word *supplices* ("we *humbly* pray"). In addition it is an expression of surrender to and union with Christ. The signs of the cross which follow were evoked by the prayer for the blessing of the offerings which is, in fact, a prayer for their consecration; the priest makes three in saying the three synonymous terms which designate them (*dona, munera, sancta sacrificia illibata*). Formerly, on account of the great quantity of the offerings, he made one sign of the cross in the middle, one to the right and one to the left.

The holy sacrifice is offered for the whole Church; petition is made for her peace and unity on the inspiration of our Lord himself in the priestly prayer which he said before giving himself up to his enemies: "Father, . . . that they should all be one, as we are one . . . so they may be perfectly made one" (John 17. 21–3). The first generations of Christians prayed constantly for the whole Church; the *Didache* (9.4 and 10.5) shows this clearly; St Polycarp, the famous martyr of Smyrna in 155 or 156, prayed aloud "for all the Catholic Church spread about over all the earth" before being delivered up to the stake. The same theme constantly recurs; it is to be found in similar terms in the prayer preparatory to the kiss of peace and in the first of the solemn prayers on Good Friday. Mention of the pope and the bishop is a very proper insistence on the hierarchical constitution of the Church; it goes back to at least the fifth century. Before St Pius V the reigning monarch was often named at this point; this is still the practice in Belgium. The last phrase concerns all the bishops of the Church and is at the same time a protestation of orthodoxy.

Prayers of intercession are inserted here; the real continuation of the petition for the acceptance of the offerings formulated in the *Te igitur* is the *Quam oblationem*.

MEMENTO OF THE LIVING

In the *Memento* the priest asks for the application of the fruit of the Mass to the intention of those for whom he intends specially to pray and for all those present.

Remember, Lord, thy servants N. and N. and all here present, whose faith and devotion are known to thee, and for whom we offer, or who themselves offer up this sacrifice in praise of thee, on behalf of themselves and all who are theirs, for the redemption of their souls, to gain the hope of safety and well-being, and who pay homage to thee, their living, true, eternal God.

We have here a relic of the diptychs. Innocent I's letter to Decentius assumes that the priest at Mass read a list of names; the practice must have been even more ancient for it seems to be mentioned in Tertullian and St Cyprian. It was certainly in general use at the beginning of the fourth century; the living and the dead were named, those who offered the Mass, the pope, bishops, the clergy, benefactors and leading laymen. The names were written on tablets in two columns, or diptychs, derived from the richly ornamented articles of the same nature used for note-taking and exchanged as presents among persons of importance. Inscription on the diptychs soon came to be a proof of orthodoxy and a title of honour; the names of those who were judged unworthy or those with whom it was desired to break off communion were effaced from the diptychs. In the west especial importance was attached to the names of the living and the dead were not mentioned in the public service; in the east, where the offering of bread and wine by the faithful disappeared at an earlier date, greater importance was attached to the list of the dead.

Outside Rome, at least, the diptychs were often read aloud by the deacon; perhaps at the same time the celebrant read the *Communicantes* which after our Lady, enumerates the apostles and popes and thus forms a kind of episcopal diptych. Prayers said simultaneously by priest and deacon are still in use in the Byzantine liturgy. The faithful were proud of having their names read in the diptychs, and on occasion would go so far as to write their names on the altar or in the margins of the sacramentaries. In order to do away with abuses of this kind Charlemagne suppressed in Gaul the reading aloud of the diptychs and his empire followed the Roman custom of commemorating the names in silence.

Were the diptychs in the primitive Roman liturgy read at the offertory as was done in other liturgies? It is a difficult question to decide and historians offer various interpretations of Innocent I's letter to Decentius which is relied upon for a solution of the difficulty. Dom Botte considers that the

Memento occupied its present place even before the time of St Gregory. The priest joins his hands as he mentions the names and prays for a moment in silence.

The text of the *Memento* requires little commentary. It assumes that those who are mentioned possess a living faith and are actively religious in their lives. Those included under "for whom we offer" are possibly the donors of foundations, thus assimilated to the offerers, or else we have here a relic of the unfortunate neglect of the rôle of the faithful as offerers which the words that follow tend to emphasize. The sacrifice of praise—for that is what the Mass is pre-eminently—is offered both for them and for all those dear to them in order to obtain the salvation of their souls, but also their safety and well-being, that is their bodily health : the Roman liturgy —ever human and realist—often mentions the humble necessities of our earthly life. The last phrase re-echoes the beginning of the prayer : those for whom we pray are assumed to send up their own fervent prayers to the living, true and eternal God.

COMMUNICANTES

The *Communicantes* is a continuation of the *Memento* : we assert our unity of fellowship with the Church triumphant and "we reverence the memory" of the saints, some of whom enjoy the great honour of being mentioned here. The fundamental notion of the mystical body and of the "ecclesial" community is here given further notable expression.

With obvious enthusiasm mention is first made of "the glorious ever-Virgin Mary, Mother of our God and Lord Jesus Christ". The expression "Mother of our God" is an indication of a later period than the Council of Ephesus which, in 431, defined Mary's divine maternity and was followed by the building in Rome of St Mary Major under Sixtus III (432–40).[1] There follow the names of the twelve apostles (all

[1] The oriental liturgies on several occasions give praise to our Lady, often in lyrical language.

save St Matthias) and of twelve martyrs held in special honour in Rome. The list of the apostles is not entirely in accordance with the order followed in the New Testament; it is the same in the Litany of Saints: the names follow their order as it is in the calendar, except for St James the Greater and St Thomas. Among the martyrs the popes Linus, Cletus, Clement, Sixtus and Cornelius are mentioned in the first place, then come Cyprian of Carthage, a contemporary of Cornelius, and the deacon Lawrence, held in special veneration in Rome. The last names are those of Chrysogonus, John and Paul, Cosmas and Damian whose churches in Rome date only from the time of Symmachus at the beginning of the sixth century; scarcely anything is known of them save their names and that they were martyrs. It is probable that the list was definitively settled by St Gregory. Only martyrs were publicly venerated in those days; the sole exception to this rule was our Lady.

The greater festivals—Christmas, Epiphany, Maundy Thursday, Easter, Ascension and Whitsun—add after the word *Communicantes* a short reminder of the mystery being celebrated. The formulas are succinct, entirely in the Roman manner. Thus that for the Epiphany reads: "We celebrate that most sacred day on which thy only-begotten Son, co-eternal with thee in thy glory, showed himself before men's eyes in the reality of our mortal flesh."

These insertions, although they are beautiful and ancient, give the effect of being an addition and impair somewhat the unity of the prayer. To the list of martyrs there have sometimes been added local saints who were the object of special devotion (e.g. St Hilary, St Martin, St Augustine, St Benedict) thus giving rise to the term "canonization"—which subsequently assumed another signification—to designate the insertion of a saint's name in the canon.

After the list of saints has been recited the intercession of all the saints is sought with the hope of obtaining at all times the help of divine protection.

HANC IGITUR

This prayer is of uncertain date; it may be conjectured, however, that it was added before the pontificate of Vigilius (c. 538). Originally it expressed a special intention in more precise terms than the *Memento*; this is still the case for Easter and Pentecost (special intention for the newly baptized) and at the consecration of bishops.[1] The first part used to vary very greatly, and the special intentions of the faithful were not always expressed very felicitously. St Gregory put an end to abuses by requiring the use of the present form of the prayer, invariable save on the three occasions mentioned above, and he added the part of the sentence referring to peace. Dom Botte has put forward the hypothesis that the *Memento* and *Hanc igitur* were said simultaneously by deacon and priest.[2]

The following is a translation of this prayer:

And so, Lord, we thy servants, and likewise thy whole household, make this peace-offering which we entreat thee to accept. Order our days in thy peace, and command that we be rescued from eternal damnation and numbered with the flock of thy elect: through Christ our Lord. Amen.

The servants here mentioned are the celebrant and his assistants who in Mass perform divine service in its highest form—that is the meaning of the word liturgy; the whole of God's household, the whole Church joins with them in the offering made at the altar. The petition for peace was motivated by the troublous times in which St Gregory lived; the prayer passes at once to the thought of eternity and of Christ's flock with which it asks that we may be numbered.

Originally the *Hanc igitur* was recited while the celebrant bowed low. Since the fifteenth century he is directed to stretch

[1] On Maundy Thursday the institution of the Eucharist is commemorated without the formulation of a special intention for any person in particular.

[2] *Le Canon de la messe romaine*, pp. 58–9; Jungmann disagrees: *op. cit.*, II, 237.

out his hands over the host and chalice, and this gesture was ordered by Pius V. Some liturgists have wondered whether it was an ancient practice which, having fallen into desuetude, was restored in the Middle Ages. The *anaphora* of St Hippolytus assumes that the bishop and his clergy stretch out their hands over the offerings. In any case, no other meaning can be attached to the gesture than that of one designating the gifts. In the Old Testament (Exod. 29. 10; Levit. 1. 4) hands were laid on the head of the victim to show that the offerer substituted it and sacrificed it in place of himself. Here the symbolism is analogous.

QUAM OBLATIONEM

We now come to a text which is also to be found equivalently in the *De Sacramentis* and so formed part of the fourth-century Roman Canon. It is the same in the case of the three prayers which follow the consecration and thus form one with it.

> We pray thee, God, be pleased to make this same offering wholly blessed, to consecrate it and approve it, making it reasonable and acceptable, so that it may become for us the body and blood of thy dearly beloved Son, our Lord Jesus Christ.

The tenor of this prayer is scarcely different from that of a secret; it is the final preparation, the last formula of oblation which concludes with the petition for consecration. The offering is primarily the bread and the wine, and, in addition, Christian people who also ought to be an offering pleasing to God (such, in the ninth century, was the opinion of Paschasius Radbertus), but the reservation mentioned in the section on the offertory should be borne in mind: the only real victim is Christ.

God is asked to bless the offering—approved means placed to our credit and, so to say, duly recorded—making it reasonable and acceptable, not merely materially but spiritually, in accordance with St Paul's remarks in Romans (12. 1) and altogether worthy of pleasing God. This heaping up of epithets shows how urgent in tone the prayer becomes. It arrives at its culminating point and conclusion in the explicit request for the transubstantiation to be effected[1]: "may this offering become for us the body and blood of thy dearly beloved Son". This last expression shows traces of an emotional tendency by no means out of place at the beginning of the mystery; as he pronounces this blessed Name the priest raises and then joins his hands in a gesture of great tenderness. Five signs of the cross are made at the words "blessed.", "body" and "blood". The three first used to be made over altar breads destined for the faithful and the others over the priest's personal oblation. The hands are always joined before making the sign of the cross over objects; it is a kind of silent prayer added to the words.

Can we see in the *Quam oblationem* a former epiclesis which has been displaced and from which the invocation of the Holy Spirit has disappeared? A text from Gelasius, quoted by Jungmann, might, if it were clearer, incline one to think so. In fact, we are obliged to admit that we do not know.[2] In the eastern liturgies it is otherwise; at the outset, possibly, they possessed a prayer not unlike the *Quam oblationem*, but since the fourth century development has taken place and they now contain a formal petition that the Holy Spirit (sometimes the Word) should come and make of the bread and wine the body and blood of Christ; this prayer occurs sometimes before and sometimes after the consecration which raises a problem that will be mentioned later in dealing with the prayer *Supplices*.

Following the simple and straightforward request of the *Quam oblationem* the great mystery is accomplished.

---

[1] Transubstantiation is the conversion, effected by the consecration, of the substance of the bread and of the wine into that of the body and blood of Christ, the appearances or accidents remaining unchanged.

[2] See Jungmann, *op. cit.,* II, 187–8.

QUI PRIDIE: THE CONSECRATION

In all liturgies the narrative of the institution forms the core of the eucharistic prayer; but it is certainly not a mere narrative for it effects what it signifies. The *Quam oblationem* has already expressed the clear intention of effectively renewing what our Saviour himself did. To each word is now joined an action which emphasizes it in order to reproduce as perfectly as possible Christ's own actions; only the fraction and the communion are postponed till later. The priest effaces himself, therefore, behind the person of Christ who speaks through his mouth, or rather between them there is established a mysterious concelebration.

The text is practically as it is to be found in the *De Sacramentis* and is common to all western liturgies, a fact that is the more remarkable since they show notable divergencies in other places. In the east there are differences of detail. The text of the Roman canon does not entirely resemble any of the four accounts of the institution in the New Testament; it represents very possibly an even older tradition; the Eucharist had already been celebrated for something like a quarter of a century when, in 55 or 56, St Paul wrote his account of the Lord's Supper in his first letter to the Corinthians.

The liturgical account begins with a relative pronoun (*Qui*, who) which connects it with the name of Christ at the end of *Quam oblationem*:

> Who, on the day before he suffered death, took bread into his holy and worshipful hands, and lifting up his eyes to thee, God, his almighty Father in heaven, and giving thanks to thee, he blessed it, broke it, and gave it to his disciples, saying: Take, all of you, and eat of this, FOR THIS IS MY BODY.

> In like manner, when he had supped, taking also this goodly cup into his holy and worshipful hands, and giving thanks to thee, he blessed it, and gave it to his disciples, saying: Take, all of you, and drink of this, FOR THIS IS THE CHALICE OF MY BLOOD, OF THE NEW AND EVERLASTING COVENANT, A MYSTERY OF FAITH.

IT SHALL BE SHED FOR YOU AND FOR MANY OTHERS, SO THAT SINS
MAY BE FORGIVEN. Whenever you shall do these things, you
shall do them in memory of me.

The words "on the day before he suffered death" are proper
to the western liturgies; the eastern liturgies follow St Paul
at this point and say, "on the night when he was being betrayed". The addition "holy and worshipful hands" is not in
Scripture but is a reverent expression of a profoundly religious
feeling. "Lifting up his eyes" is also a feature of two out-
standing miracles—the multiplication of loaves, a figure of the
Eucharist (Mark 6. 41) and the raising of Lazarus (John
11. 41). The form of consecration of the bread is the same
as in Matthew (26. 26) and partly as in 1 Corinthians (11. 24)
save for the phrase "given up for you".

For the chalice, qualified as "goodly",[1] the text follows St
Paul (1 Cor. 11. 25) and St Luke (22. 20) with the addition
of a few details in order to render the two consecrations
symmetrical in form. The reference to the new Covenant and
the redemptive nature of the Last Supper is to be found in all
four New Testament accounts. The command to repeat the
rite thus accomplished is mentioned only by St Paul and St
Luke. All liturgies include it.

Mysterium fidei, mystery of faith, may well be a reference
to St Paul's epistle to Timothy (1 Tim. 3. 9). It is only a
parenthesis but adds to the solemnity of the formula which,
for the chalice, attains the desired proportion. It is to be found
in the Gelasian and Gregorian sacramentaries. The twofold
mention of thanksgiving by our Lord has led to the name of
Eucharist being given to the whole Mass. The two signs of
the cross were included because of the word *benedixit* (he
blessed); here, in the very act of sacrifice, they fall naturally
into place.

With the twofold consecration the great mystery is effected.
Christ is present on the altar as really as at the Last Supper
and on Calvary, with the same dispositions of offering and

[1] Cf. Psalm 22. 5.

love, under appearances and with the use of formulas which vividly recall his sacrifices with the shedding of his blood. Adoration from the depths of our hearts is here required as is very aptly suggested by the rite of elevation. The gifts laid upon the altar have been accepted by God and have become the body and blood of Christ, and it is he, the only efficacious Victim, who now offers himself by the ministry of the Church. The Church, inseparable from her Head, now offers herself together with him. It remains only for her to make explicit, in so far as it is hers, the offering of the divine Victim which, finally, she will receive in communion. All the faithful, in union with her, should make their own the redemptive sacrifice of Christ, offer Christ and offer themselves for the glory of the Holy Trinity. This, an act of the virtue of religion, is the primary consideration; concern for our own spiritual profit comes afterwards.

THE ELEVATION

The elevation immediately after the consecration is a medieval rite which emphasizes the fundamental moment of sacrifice by showing the sacred elements for the adoration of the faithful.

In all liturgies there is an elevation before the communion in order that the faithful may adore the Blessed Sacrament before they receive it. In the Roman rite it occurs at the final doxology of the canon before the Lord's Prayer. Until the introduction of the new order of Holy Week services, on Good Friday it immediately preceded the fraction and the communion. Before giving the host to the faithful it is always held up before them with the words "Behold the Lamb of God" (*Ecce Agnus Dei*). Since about the fourth century this has been the practice in the east.

In the twelfth century in taking the bread for consecration the priest raised it high enough for the people to be able to see it. Bishops, Eudes of Paris especially, in about 1210, ordered the host to be held only breast-high and to be raised higher only after the words of consecration, lest the people should adore it too soon. It concerned therefore regulation of, and emphasis on, a gesture already in use, the emphasis being provoked by the especial religious value attached in those days to seeing the host. The desire to see the host is a characteristic devotion of the period closely connected with the great love which developed in those days for the sacred humanity of Christ and with the growing practice of spiritual communion since, unfortunately, sacramental communion had become rare. St Louis who was present every day at one or more Masses only communicated six times a year. Eucharistic miracles supplied a similar emphasis.

A secondary factor in the development of the elevation may well have been the reaction against an error which taught that the bread was consecrated only after the words of consecration had been said over the chalice; this false doctrine was held especially by two doctors of the University of Paris, contemporaries of Eudes, Peter the Cantor and Peter Comestor.[1] The elevation directly after the words had been said over the bread cut short this strange theological speculation.

The rite of elevation spread rapidly and soon assumed extreme importance for the faithful; superstition was sometimes mixed with it. Those who had not seen the elevation imagined that they had not heard Mass. Sometimes people came to church merely for that, not always quietly and pushing their way in; lessons in school were interrupted for the children to be taken to see the elevation. The congregation in some places called out to the priest, telling him to hold the host up higher. In English churches a bell, called the Sanctus bell, was rung to warn those in the neighbourhood, or else the server opened a low window in the wall near the altar and rang a hand bell.

Originally the priest bowed after each consecration; genuflection scarcely appeared before the fifteenth century and was made obligatory by Pius V. The elevation led to a certain

---

[1] He was a glutton (*comestor*) for books not food.

number of secondary rites such as the third candle lighted at the *Sanctus* and left burning until the communion, the torch bearers, the bell to warn the congregation, the ringing of the church bell to allow those unable to come to church to make an act of faith, incensing of the Blessed Sacrament and the singing of hymns in honour of the Eucharist after the elevation. It is probably the desire to see the host that is at the origin of exposition and benediction of the Blessed Sacrament and the Corpus Christi procession; it resulted in an extraordinary development of devotion to the real Presence and eucharistic adoration. Reverence gradually prevailed over the desire to see the host and many no longer raised their eyes at the elevation; it was Pius X who reminded the faithful of the meaning of the elevation and called on them once more to look at the host.

The elevation of the chalice was introduced in the fourteenth century by analogy with the elevation of the host and was only made obligatory by Pius V's Missal. There was not the same reason for it; the Precious Blood cannot be seen and there is the danger of spilling it. A certain devotion to the chalice itself came to be associated with the practice.

Outside penitential seasons an unobtrusive organ accompaniment is allowed, but it would seem that complete silence is more reverent; in a large and well-behaved congregation it produces a profound and religious impression.

THE ANAMNESIS[1]: UNDE ET MEMORES

And now, Lord, we thy servants, and with us all thy holy people, calling to mind the blessed Passion of this same Christ, thy Son, our Lord, likewise his resurrection from the grave, and glorious ascension into heaven, offer to thy sovereign majesty, out of the gifts thou hast bestowed upon us, a sacrifice that is pure, holy and unblemished, the sacred Bread of everlasting life, and the Cup of eternal salvation.

[1] *Anamnesis* is the transcription of a Greek word meaning memorial.

This and the two following prayers are common to all liturgies, at least equivalently, and by inspiration must go back to apostolic times. They are elements belonging to the ancient Roman canon and their text in its present form was probably fixed in the fourth century. They constitute the offering, the setting before God of the sacrifice effected on the altar. The scheme on which they are fashioned is easy to perceive: offering of the victim present on the altar, recommendation of the victim to God by recalling the sacrifices of the old Law which were most acceptable to him, a request that the victim may be received and for a share in the fruits of the sacrifice. They emphasize the offering of Christ and at the same time make it an act of the Church—"we . . . offer". The priestly function of the Church, begun at the offertory, reaches its climax now that her gifts have become the body and blood of Christ, the only offering worthy of Christ.

The prayer *Unde et memores* is called by the Greeks *anamnesis* because it states that the Church acts in memory of our Lord and in accordance with his formal command, "Do this in memory". The Church is mindful of this and nothing is more moving than this assertion of fidelity to Christ's express command. Other terms are to be found in early Latin authors: "after the mysteries" (*post mysteria*), "invocation after the mysteries" (*invocatio post mysteria*), "completion of the mystery" (*confirmatio sacramenti*) etc.

The word "servants" refers to the celebrant and the clergy assisting him, in the same way as above at the *Hanc igitur*. The faithful join with him and also the whole Church thus exercising what St Peter calls the royal priesthood (1 Peter 2. 9).

There follows a list of the mysteries of Christ which are commemorated. The Roman canon confines itself to the passion, resurrection and ascension, the three of primary importance. The nativity is to be found in some texts which are no earlier than the ninth century; it is doubtful whether they are derived from the primitive anamnesis. The Greek liturgy concludes with mention of the second coming, an obvious allusion to the words of St Paul: "So it is the Lord's death that you are heralding, whenever you eat this bread and drink this cup, until he comes" (1 Cor. 11. 26). There is ample justification for these additions but the mysteries named in the Roman canon may well suffice: does not the passion presuppose the Incarnation which preceded it?

The holy sacrifice is offered principally in memory of the passion, as St Thomas states in the collect that he composed for Corpus Christi. The passion sealed in the blood of Christ the new and eternal covenant reconciling humanity with God and forgiving sins; that is why we dare to speak of the "blessed passion": this same sacrifice of Christ is mysteriously continued on the altar; only the manner of offering is different, says the Council of Trent. The redemptive sacrifice, the offering of Calvary, continues in an unbloody manner. The vivifying death of Christ is really heralded and proclaimed; his merits are poured out over men. In the strongest sense of the word there is *representation*, that is, effective presence made sensible by the host and chalice and by the words of consecration.[1]

There is this to be added. Our Saviour's passion was a triumphant victorious death, sanctioned, so to say, by the resurrection, the pre-eminent proof of the divinity of Christ and of the acceptance of his sacrifice by the Father and a guarantee of the efficacy of the redemption. The Christ of Easter can die no more and it is he who comes upon the altar, although his glory remains hidden. In union with his resurrection he pours out over the world the merits of his passion and brings to mankind the divine life which he possesses in its fullness. The resurrection and passion are inseparable and are commemorated together at Mass. It is noticeable that the liturgy of Holy Week does not mention one without the other; read, for example, the collects of Palm Sunday and

[1] In the rite of Lyon the priest says this prayer with arms outstretched in the form of a cross.

Maundy Thursday. In communion we receive the true body, once sacrificed on the cross, but it is the living and glorious body of the risen and victorious Christ, raised up on Ascension Day to the right hand of the Father where he reigns for ever and continues to exercise his priesthood by interceding for us and prolonging the sublime sacrifice of Calvary. The ascension, the crown of the passion and resurrection, is therefore also commemorated at Mass. The whole mystery of redemption, the whole paschal mystery, is included in it; the entire work of our salvation is there continued.

The second part of the prayer, the oblation in the proper sense of the word, is one of the solemn moments of the liturgical action: we offer, the Church offers, the victim made present by the consecration. This offering is derived from God's gifts; we can give nothing to our Creator which he has not himself previously given to us, whether it be the humble produce of man's work and the material support of his life or, *a fortiori*, the body and blood of our Lord. Everything comes from him and yet we have the right to say that *we offer*, that the offering is ours, for we have prepared it and brought it to the altar and it is one of us who has pronounced the words which have made it the body and blood of Christ. This idea is to be found in all the ancient liturgies; it is moving in its humility which acknowledges God's sovereign rights yet by no means minimizes the sacrificial act of the Church.

The prayer of offering concludes with reverent, sincere praise of the victim offered: a perfectly pure victim to the exclusion of all other, a holy victim even to the extent of making souls holy (this the victims of the Old Law could not do), an unblemished victim, Christ the innocent, the sinless, the sacred bread and the cup which gives everlasting life, as our Saviour promised (John 6. 51, 54). The unpretentious offering of bread and wine, a symbol of the offering that the Church makes of herself, has been transformed by the transubstantiation which has integrated her sacrifice with Christ's.

The signs of the cross which occur here, like all those following the consecration, have aroused a certain amount of discussion. Some of the Fathers at the Council of Trent would
have preferred to see them eliminated. Several explanations
have been put forward: some have seen them as simple
gestures designating the offerings, or as reminders of the
passion, or else as a result of the custom of making the sign
of the cross at words that imply sacrifice—body, blood, bless,
etc.—continued after the consecration. A less superficial
interpretation would seem to be called for.

Throughout the canon the Church treats the host as a sacrament, asks God to receive and accept it and continuously
makes the sign of the cross over it—not unfittingly in a rite
which is a prolongation among us of Christ's sacrifice. The
eucharistic prayer obtains the transubstantiation from God, and
until the Middle Ages little concern was shown over the precise
moment at which it occurred. Our signs of the cross, therefore,
are real blessings. God is asked to change the bread and wine
into the body and blood of Christ throughout the prayer which
takes, of course, a certain time. God grants this favour at a
moment which is not the last, that is, when the words of
institution are said. Nevertheless, it is in virtue of the whole
prayer that the divine action is accomplished; the transubstantiation is the effect of the whole anaphora regarded as
indivisible. As it cannot all be said at once it so happens
that what has already been granted is asked for afterwards;
the order of the requests is of little importance. The same
explanation applies to the post-consecratory epiclesis in some
rites. In support of this view the analogy of priestly ordination
may be cited; the powers of celebrating Mass and absolving
sins are declared to be given after being already conferred by
the laying on of hands and the preface, the matter and the
form respectively of the sacrament.

No liturgy adds to mention of the ascension that of the
descent of the Holy Spirit though it would appear to be natural
to do so; liturgies which have an epiclesis, however, usually

place it at this point. The anamneses are always of great interest; many give clear teaching of the real presence like that of
the Roman canon. It has been conjectured that certain secrets
in which the offering of Christ is clearly stated (Epiphany,
seventh Sunday after Pentecost) are ancient anamneses trans-
posed to before the preface.

SUPRA QUAE PROPITIO

After the oblation comes the request that the Church's offering may be acceptable to God as, in the Old Testament, were
three offerings which were remarkable for the dispositions
accompanying them. Each of them is a figure of Christ's
sacrifice.

> Deign to regard them with a favourable and gracious coun-
> tenance, and to accept them as thou wast pleased to accept
> the offerings of thy good servant Abel, and the sacrifice of our
> father Abraham, and that which thy great priest Melchisedech
> sacrificed to thee, a holy offering, a victim without blemish.

Abel's offering was that of an innocent man who reverently
sacrificed to God the first fruits of his flock (Gen. 4. 4); God
accepted his faith and his gifts (Heb. 11. 4). Abraham's sacrifice was an extraordinary act of obedience and faith (Gen. 22);
the order to sacrifice his son seemed to destroy God's promise
to him of posterity; but God did not require the completion
of the sacrifice and by the reiteration of his promises rewarded
the heroism of him whom very properly we call our patriarch,
the father of all who imitate his faith (Gal. 3. 7; Heb. 11.
17–19). Lastly, the mysterious Melchisedech is called priest of
"the most high God" in Genesis (14. 18); his priesthood is a
figure of Christ's (Ps. 109; Heb. 7) and his offering of bread
and wine of the Eucharist. The last words—"a holy offering,
a victim without blemish"—were added by St Leo as a protest
against the Manichean heresy which regarded matter, and
especially wine, as evil.

If these offerings were accepted, with all the more reason is Christ's pleasing to God. It could not be otherwise; but the Church asks that, in so far as it is her own offering, it may be regarded with favour. God will accept it "with a favourable and gracious countenance" if it is accompanied by dispositions as pure as those of the Patriarchs. This condition is always fulfilled by the universal Church in whose name the sacrifice is offered; we ask that it may be so in the case of all those who are proximately associated with it.

SUPPLICES: PROBLEM OF THE EPICLESIS

The prayer of offering concludes with a third formula which, in the *De Sacramentis*, forms one with that which precedes it.

Humbly we ask it of thee, God almighty; bid these things be carried by the hands of thy holy angel up to thy altar on high, before the face of thy divine majesty, so that those of us who by taking part in the sacrifice of this altar shall have received the sacred body and blood of thy Son, may be filled with every grace and heavenly blessing. Through the same Christ our Lord.

Amen.

The Church asks that her offering may be carried up to the heavenly altar. The body and blood of Christ are in heaven, and consequently have not to be presented to God; but in so far as they constitute our sacrifice and are offered by us, they need to be accepted by him. The meaning of the offering is therefore the same as in the *Supra quae*: the efficacy of Christ's sacrifice for our own souls depends on our dispositions; we ask God to receive our sacrifice and to inspire us with fitting sentiments to participate in it by communion with the maximum of fruitfulness.

The heavenly altar is a metaphor signifying God in his acceptance of our offering united to our Saviour's. Christ never ceases to make intercession for us and to present to his Father the merits of his sacrifice effected by the shedding of his blood;

this is the meaning of the vision of the Lamb who was slain
(Apoc. 5. 7). The offering of Christ, present in heaven in his
glorious body, is uninterrupted; it forms the apex and is the
foundation of the unity of all the Masses celebrated on earth;
it is a continuation of the acceptance by God of the redemptive
sacrifice. But the Church must give and offer before receiving;
the abundance of graces for the communicants is subordinate
to God's acceptance of the Church's offering, hence the importance of the dispositions in which the holy sacrifice is
offered by us.

The identity of the angel who is to carry the Church's offering to heaven has given rise to some discussion. Some have
taken the view that it is Christ, others the Holy Spirit; it is
probable that it refers to an angel in the proper sense of the
word. The text of *De Sacramentis* which uses the plural ("by
the hands of your holy angels") provides strong confirmation
of this interpretation. But which angel is it? The archangel
Michael has been suggested, but the unnamed angel who, in
the Apocalypse (8. 3–4), offers to God the prayers of the Saints
on the golden altar placed before his throne seems to have
inspired the terms of the *Supplices* and provides the best
explanation.

The request for every grace and heavenly blessing refers to
those who are to communicate and shows clearly that, in the
mind of the Church, all who are present at Mass should take
part in it sacramentally.

The "taking part in the sacrifice of this altar" is another way
of saying eating of the victim there offered; St Paul uses similar
language (Heb. 13. 10; compare with 1 Cor. 9. 13; 10. 18). No
distinction is now made between the earthly altar and the
heavenly altar and our thoughts turn naturally towards the
second aspect of the eucharistic celebration, the sacrificial
meal in which the offerers are invited to God's table to eat of
the victim. The conclusion "Through the same Christ our
Lord" might be followed immediately by *Per quem haec
omnia*, and then by the fraction and the communion if further

prayers of intercession were not included in the present canon. The *Supplices* is the culminating point of the offering and of the priestly prayer of the Church, the formal request for definitive acceptance by God. The profound bow and the kissing of the altar emphasize the intensity of prayer. We ask God that our sacrifice may not be as a burnt offering in which the victim was entirely consumed, but that the victim sacrificed and taken up to heaven may be given back to us in heavenly blessings by the communion. Thus the sacrifice will be both acceptable to God and beneficial to man, a sacrifice of thanksgiving and of covenant. This very simple notion is in perfect agreement with the New Testament and the ancient liturgical texts. In a sort of immense parabola the line of our prayer rises up from earth to heaven and then comes back again, laden with divine gifts at the communion.

The literary structure of the *Supplices* is somewhat complex and raises a final problem, that of the epiclesis.[1]

The first words of the prayer (*Supplices te rogamus*) occur several times in the postcommunions of the Gregorian sacramentary. The second part, a petition for the taking up of our offering to heaven, comes from the *De Sacramentis*.

The last part is the conclusion of an epiclesis which has been adapted, for it does not invoke the intervention of the Holy Spirit to effect the consecration. There is, therefore, no epiclesis in the proper sense of the term in our Roman canon. After the fourth century it is otherwise in the oriental liturgies. St Cyril, Bishop of Jerusalem, instructed the newly baptized in these terms: "Then, having sanctified ourselves by these spiritual hymns, we call upon the merciful God to send forth his Holy Spirit upon the gifts lying before him; that he may make the bread the body of Christ and the wine the blood of Christ".[2]

[1] From two Greek words meaning "call" and "upon". The Holy Spirit is *called down* upon the offerings.

[2] *Mystagogical Catecheses*, 5. 7. See F. L. Cross, *St. Cyril's Lectures on the Christian Sacraments* (S.P.C.K., London, and Macmillan, New York, 1951), p. 74.

The various formulas of epiclesis ultimately came to be misunderstood and caused it to be regarded by several eastern theologians, especially St John Damascene, as necessary for consecration on a par with the words of institution. The Orthodox, after the seventeenth century, even assert that the epiclesis alone suffices. The liturgy of St John Chrysostom, nowadays in use by many eastern Christians in union with Rome as well as by the Orthodox, after the narrative of the Last Supper use formulas, in themselves very beautiful, which would seem at first sight to uphold this view :

Lord, who at the third hour sent your Holy Spirit upon the apostles, take him not away from us, you who are merciful, but renew him in us who pray to you.

Deacon. Sir, bless the holy bread.

Priest. And make this bread the precious body of thy Christ.

Deacon. Amen. Sir, bless the holy cup.

Priest. And that which is in this chalice the precious blood of thy Christ.

Deacon. Amen. Sir, bless both holy gifts.

Priest. Changing them by thy Holy Spirit.

Deacon. Amen. Amen. Amen. Reverend Sir, remember me a sinner.

Priest. That they may bring to them that partake spiritual cleansing, forgiveness of sins, indwelling of thy Holy Spirit, fulfilment of the kingdom of heaven, confidence towards thee, and neither judgement nor condemnation.

The liturgy of St Basil contains an almost similar epiclesis.

Catholic theology asserts, nevertheless, that the doctrine attributing the consecration to the words of institution and not to the epiclesis is the only one really founded on tradition; this is justified by abundant patristic evidence, both eastern and western.

In the description of the Eucharist (already quoted) St Justin states that the body and blood of Christ are "a food consecrated by the formula of prayer which comes from him". St Irenaeus (*Adversus haereses* 5. 2. 2) speaks in the same way.

In the fourth century St Athanasius teaches that the bread and wine become the body and blood of Christ when the "great and prodigious prayers" are said; in the context there can be no doubt of what is meant. The *De Sacramentis*, a little later is categoric: "What words effect the consecration and whose are they? The words of the Lord Jesus . . . When the moment comes at which this venerable sacrament is effected the bishop speaks no longer in his own person, he uses the words of Christ. Therefore the word of Christ effects the sacrament."

It should be noticed, in addition, that in certain ancient liturgical documents the epiclesis is sometimes absent, and that in other cases it is addressed to the Word; on occasion, although addressed to the Holy Spirit it is placed before the words of institution, or else it asks the Holy Spirit, not to effect the consecration but to ensure the fruits of communion; this last case is that of the anaphora of St Hippolytus. The position is a complicated one, therefore, and even the *epicleses* addressed to the Holy Spirit do not always reveal a consecratory intention.

On several occasions the Byzantines have discussed with Rome the question of the efficacy of the epiclesis. The decree for the Armenians and the Council of Trent have both stated that the consecration is effected by the words of institution; that is a certain truth and one *proximum fidei*, but it has not been directly defined.[1]

How then are the Byzantine epicleses to be explained?

In the first place it should be noticed that in these liturgies after each consecration occur acclamations ("Amen, Amen!") which leave no doubt at all concerning the efficacy of the words of institution. St John Chrysostom himself on more than one occasion clearly gives his views on this subject: "The priest takes Christ's place when he utters these words . . . He

---

[1] A truth which is *proximum fidei* is so called because it appears to follow from infallible decisions of the Church without being explicitly formulated.

says, 'This is my body'. This statement transforms the gifts which have been brought . . . and effects the perfect sacrifice." The introduction of an apparently consecratory epiclesis after the narrative of the Last Supper is due to a desire to follow in the anaphora the order of the interventions by the Son and the Holy Spirit in the redemption of mankind. The invocation of the Holy Spirit had therefore to be placed after the account of the institution, just as Pentecost followed the passion and resurrection. In addition, although transubstantiation takes place in an instant, that, namely of the recital of the words of institution, it is impossible to say everything at once. Consecration, oblation of the sacrifice and the request for its acceptance by God, are effectively realized when the priest pronounces the words of institution; but the statement of the thoughts developed in the anamnesis requires a certain time and can only come afterwards. The consecration effects the transubstantiation; the epiclesis states how it is effected, namely by the action of the Holy Spirit in conjunction with the Father and the Son.

The presence of the epiclesis after the words of institution should occasion no surprise since for a considerable period no attempt was made to determine the precise moment of consecration, as was pointed out above in connection with the prayer *Unde et memores*. It was known that consecration was effected by the anaphora and no more was asked; similarly, with the administration of the sacrament of penance the exact moment of the forgiveness of sins was left uncertain. Consequently, the position of the epiclesis was of little importance. Theological development in the Middle Ages provided a more exact statement which enabled the significance of the epiclesis to be better understood, without modifying the prayers of the canon or their text.

[1] Homily I on the betrayal of Judas, 6. In Migne, *Patrologia Graeca*, 49, 380.

THE MEMENTO OF THE DEAD

The *Memento* of the dead and the *Nobis quoque peccatoribus* form a second break in the primitive canon and constitute the continuation of the diptychs, the first part of which
preceded the consecration.

From the Christian community about to receive the body
and blood of Christ consideration now turns towards the dead
who can no longer take part in this sacrament but have not
ceased to belong to the mystical body of Christ.

> Remember also, Lord, thy servants N. and N., who have
> gone before us with the sign of faith and sleep the sleep of
> peace. To them, Lord, and to all who rest in Christ, grant, we
> entreat thee, a place of cool repose, of light and peace. Through
> the same Christ our Lord. Amen.

The *Memento* of the dead is absent from the Gelasian and
Gregorian sacramentaries and does not figure in the papal
Mass of the seventh and eighth centuries. Nevertheless, the
text is ancient in form and various documents show that a
commemoration of the dead was made at Mass in the fourth
century both in the east and the west, sometimes before and
sometimes after the consecration.[1] In Rome, until the eighth
century, it was only used in the weekday Masses celebrated for
the dead; finally it found its way into all Masses without
exception.

Why is this second *Memento* not joined to the first? Various
hypotheses have been suggested but lack any textual warrantry.
Some have supposed that a desire to avoid confusion between
the dead honoured as saints and those for whom prayers were
offered caused this separation into two distinct lists; it has
also been conjectured that as the reading of the diptychs was
often a lengthy proceeding it was interrupted at the end of the
list of the living with the consequence that the list of the dead
was postponed to its present place. Dom Botte[2] is inclined to

[1] Jungmann, *op. cit.*, II, pp. 237–48.
[2] *Ordinaire de la Messe*, Paris, 1953, pp. 23–4.

admit that this *Memento* belonged to the primitive structure of the canon, perhaps as a prayer said by the deacon. But that does not explain the lack of connection between the *Memento* and the *Supplices*. The Irish Missal of Bobbio (beginning of the eighth century) is the first to insert the *Memento* at its present place.

As he says the first part of this prayer the priest slowly raises his hands then joins them and remains a moment in silent recollection with his eyes fixed on the consecrated host. The "sign of faith" means baptism; we pray, then, for those who have remained faithful to the obligations imposed by it. Jungmann suggests that it also refers to the last sacraments whose reception is a mark of Christian fidelity. The mention of peace into which the dead have entered recalls the funerary inscriptions in the catacombs where peace in Christ is a habitual theme.

The second part of the *Memento* is of universalist inspiration and very beautiful. The expression "place of cool repose" which primitively designated a funeral meal should be understood here of the happiness of heaven; the meaning is made clearer by the words "light and peace". There is no satisfactory explanation for the bow of the head prescribed at the words "Through the same Christ our Lord"; the Middle Ages, always inclined to allegory, regarded it as an illusion to Christ's attitude as he died.

The names of the dead have sometimes been read in public, as previously were those of the living, and from this practice likewise arose abuses and difficulties. A relic of the custom is to be discerned in the reading of the names of the departed from the pulpit before the sermon. The insertion of the *Memento* (both for the living and the dead) in the very heart of the canon, in which the celebrant alone is concerned, endows them both with a note of discreet and silent intimacy well in harmony with the central part of the Mass.

In any case, whatever the reasons for the insertion of the *Memento* of the dead at this point there can be no doubt that prayer for the dead and its presence during Mass is extremely ancient and is possibly the continuation of a tradition going back to apostolic times. Christian devotion is very rightly attached to intercession for the dead and the celebration of Mass for the repose of their souls.

NOBIS QUOQUE

This prayer, like the *Communicantes*, belongs approximately to the period of Symmachus for it was only then that several of the saints enumerated became the object of special veneration in Rome; it is even probable that the list was only definitively established by St Gregory.

The *Memento* of the dead is continued, with an increased note of humility, by a prayer for the celebrant and his ministers. It is the same in most liturgies.

> To us also, thy sinful servants, who put our trust in thy countless acts of mercy, deign to grant some share and fellowship with thy holy apostles and martyrs: with John, Stephen, Matthias, Barnabas, Ignatius, Alexander, Marcellinus, Peter, Felicity, Perpetua, Agatha, Lucy, Agnes, Cecily, Anastasia and all thy saints. Into their company we pray thee admit us, not weighing our deserts, but freely granting us forgiveness: through Christ our Lord.

The celebrant raises his voice for the first three words; this is the relic of a custom that has long since disappeared. The *Nobis quoque* gave the signal to the subdeacons, who had remained bowing low since the *Sanctus*, to stand upright and return to their places in order to be ready to help with the fraction directly the canon was over. The celebrant acknowledges himself a sinner and unworthy and implores God in his mercy to admit him, and the ministers assisting him, into the fellowship of the apostles and saints. The list corresponds with, and completes, that of the *Communicantes*; it mentions in the first place John (obviously here St John the Baptist) and then seven men followed by seven women, all martyrs. Stephen is the first deacon whose glorious martyrdom is recounted in the Acts of the Apostles (6. 8–7. 60). Two apostles come next: Matthias elected to take the place of Judas (Acts 1. 15–26) and left out of the first list, probably in order not to exceed the number twelve, and Barnabas, an apostle in the wide sense of the word, St Paul's companion on his first missionary journeys. Ignatius is the famous bishop of Antioch, sentenced to the wild beasts in Rome under Trajan. Besides their names and the place of their martyrdom little else is known of Alexander, Marcellinus and Peter. Perpetua and Felicity confessed the faith at Carthage (their "acts" are famous), Agatha and Lucy in Sicily. The list concludes with the names of two Roman martyrs, Agnes and Cecily, and of Anastasia, martyred at Sirmium and later honoured in Rome.

In conclusion the celebrant protests that his merits do not count beside those of the saints and implores God's pardon so that he and his assistants may be one day joined to them in heaven.

PER QUEM HAEC OMNIA

The canon properly so called concludes as follows:

> It is ever through him (i.e. Christ) that all these good gifts created by thee, Lord, are by thee sanctified, endowed with life, blessed and bestowed upon us.
>
> Through him, and with him, and in him, thou, God, almighty Father, in the unity of the Holy Spirit, hast honour and glory. World without end. Amen.

This prayer is the logical sequel to the *Supplices*; in the Gallican and Visigothic liturgies it was directly joined to it. There is some difficulty in discovering the exact meaning of the first words in the Latin text (*per quem haec omnia semper bona creas*—"it is ever . . . thee").

According to Mgr Duchesne, Cardinal Schuster and Dom Cabrol they refer to the fruits of the earth (wine, oil, fruit,

etc) that used to be blessed at this point in the Mass. Even
nowadays on Maundy Thursday the bishop blesses the oil of
the sick before beginning this prayer. But in every case a
formula distinct from the *Per quem* was used and was said
before it. It is not certain that the words *haec omnia* ("all
these") referred to what had been blessed since they were
retained at all Masses.

Lebrun and Mgr Batiffol consider that we have here a
doxology and nothing more. *Haec omnia bona* ("all these
good things") designate all creation, but especially the consecrated bread and wine which represent it and in some sort are
its first fruits. We have here, then, an acclamation to the
Father who, by his Word, creates all good things, but especially the consecrated species to which the words which follow
apply better than to anything else.

The only elevation of the ancient Mass occurred during the
final phrase and warned the faithful to prepare for communion. At *per ipsum* the archdeacon, his hands covered with
a linen cloth, raised the chalice by its handles while the pope
touched the edges with the two loaves that were his personal
offering. In this way it was intended to show the unity of the
sacrament and to emphasize that Christ present on the altar
in a state of mystical death, is nevertheless living and present
entirely under each of the elements which were brought together and united as much as possible. At the same time, the
elevation emphasized and brought out very clearly the meaning of the doxology, the highest glorification of the Holy
Trinity. Subsequently the threefold formula, "Through him,
and with him and in him" has led to the three signs of the
cross with the host from one edge to the other of the chalice,
and the mention of the divine Persons caused two others to
be made in front of the chalice. Nowadays, owing to the signs
of the cross, the elevation (the "little elevation" as it is sometimes called) is made during the last words. It is desirable that
these gestures should be made with all the solemnity possible.

The rite took its present definitive shape in the twelfth century. Before the Lord's Prayer occupied its present position the fraction must have followed immediately; until the reform of 1956 this was the practice on Good Friday: the celebrant elevated the consecrated host over the paten and then broke it.

The words of the doxology are taken in part from St Paul (Rom. 11. 36). They are majestic in their simplicity and their significance is enhanced by the signs of the cross and the elevation of the sacred species. No doxology is invested with such solemnity. The greatness, the loftiness of the formula, make it a worthy conclusion to the Roman Canon.

It forms an echo to the *Vere dignum* of the preface and is an excellent statement of the eucharistic end of sacrifice which is to give thanks to God and to glorify him by, with and in Christ. It is the most perfect homage that can be paid to the Holy Trinity. At the very moment when Christ is about to give himself to the Church in the Eucharist it is very right that the Church should express the intention of giving herself to God and should send up to him all glory by the mediation of Christ, the offerer, victim and priest. The "unity of the Holy Spirit" can probably be understood of the Church, unified and made holy by him, more probably indeed here than in the conclusion of the collects, without losing sight of the Trinitarian aspect of the formula. Jungmann puts it very well: "*In ipso* and *in unitate Spiritus Sancti* therefore designate one and the same all encompassing well-spring, whence arises the glorification of the Father, in one case viewed in relation to Christ whose mystic body the redeemed form, in the other case viewed in relation to the Spirit, whose breath inspires them."

The *Amen* said by the congregation is the only intervention by the faithful in the canon; such intervention is found only as an exception in ancient liturgies after the consecration. Evidence of it can be found in St Justin and very rightly is it renowned. It deserves to be uttered with especial devotion for it is an act of faith in the holy mysteries and the people's ratification of what has been done at the altar.[1]

[1] *Amen* is a Hebrew word which has passed unchanged into our language. It means "truly", "let it be so". It expresses assent to a prayer or the desire to see accomplished the wishes formulated (as, for example, at the end of the Lord's Prayer). In the Gospel our Lord often uses it with the meaning of "In all truth (I say to you)".

CHAPTER VIII

PARTAKING OF THE MYSTERY: COMMUNION AND THANKSGIVING

PATER AND LIBERA

After the offering of the sacrifice comes the Lord's meal, participation through the Eucharist in the life of the glorified Christ, a perfect expression of the communion of saints and a privileged means of making it more effective. The immediate preparation for communion, which is important in order to increase the soul's charity and receptivity to grace, begins with the singing of the Lord's Prayer.

The inclusion of the Lord's Prayer in Mass is found certainly in the fourth century and possibly in the third. It may have been introduced at first in those churches in which the Eucharist was celebrated every day; or as a result of the faithful reciting it before communion at home on ordinary days. A great number of the Fathers have applied to the Eucharist the petition for daily bread, although in the literal sense it refers to bread in the ordinary sense.

St Gregory speaks in obscure terms of the position that he assigned to the Lord's Prayer in the Roman Mass. Mgr Batiffol thinks that before Gregory it was not said and that he introduced it. Most modern liturgists consider (and with reason) that he merely changed its position to immediately after the canon whereas previously it had been said after the fraction.

It is noteworthy that on Good Friday, when no Mass is celebrated, the Lord's Prayer forms the principal preparation for communion; to it is added only the last of the prayers usually said after the kiss of peace. St Gregory probably placed the *Pater* immediately after the canon in order to say it at the altar and not when at his throne for the fraction. Perhaps he was influenced by Byzantine practice which he had known during his time in Constantinople. The first part of the Lord's Prayer, which desires the glory of God and the accomplishment of his will, is an excellent continuation of the canon. Jungmann remarks: "The spirit and disposition in which our Lord himself had offered up his sacrifice and which we must draw from our co-performance of it, could hardly have been expressed more cogently."[1]

In all liturgies the Lord's Prayer is preceded by a prologue or introduction similar to that in the Roman Mass: "Let us pray. Urged by our Saviour's bidding, and schooled by his divine ordinance, we make bold to say: Our Father . . ."

The profound religious atmosphere pervading the canon is augmented here with the very great reverence shown to our Saviour's own prayer. As we know, in the early Church the Lord's Prayer was only taught to the catechumens a few weeks before baptism, and outside Mass it was said in a low voice; some vestiges of this discipline have remained in the divine office. We only say it solemnly in excusing ourselves, sinners that we are, for calling God our Father, and in experiencing a certain awe at the thought of the holiness required for a sincere recitation of this divine prayer. Tertullian called the Lord's Prayer an epitome of the Gospel; it unites us with the Spirit of Christ before we partake of his body; is not the fruit of communion the realization to the fullest extent of what we ask in the Lord's Prayer?

A rubric directs the celebrant to say the Lord's Prayer with hands outstretched, as for the canon, while looking at the consecrated host; our Lord's prayer is said over the sacrament

[1] Jungmann, *op. cit.*, II, p. 279.

of his body; this is a further example of the sober poetical note of our Roman liturgy. Most oriental liturgies have retained the ancient custom, to be found also in the Gallican liturgy, of all the congregation saying the prayer aloud with the celebrant. The Mozarabic liturgy required the congregation to answer *Amen* to each petition. Elsewhere in the west, since the time of St Augustine, the Lord's Prayer has been reserved to the celebrant. The people associate themselves with it by saying the last petition. The only exception is in the new Good Friday rite in which the Lord's Prayer is said by celebrant and congregation together. Everything has been so arranged as to give this prayer a place of honour and the utmost solemnity. The rite of Lyon has an elevation of the consecrated elements at *sicut in caelo et in terra*, a less apt position than the elevation at the concluding doxology of the canon.

The Lord's Prayer is followed by the *Libera*, an embolism or expansion of the last petition which effects the transition to the *Pax Domini*. There is a similar prayer in other rites, and in the Gallican the formula varied very greatly. That of the Roman rite is as follows:

> Deliver us, we pray thee, Lord, from every evil, past, present and to come, and at the intercession of the blessed and glorious ever-virgin Mary, Mother of God, and of thy blessed apostles Peter and Paul, of Andrew, and of all the saints, be pleased to grant peace in our days, so that with the manifold help of thy compassion we may be ever free from sin and safe from all disquiet. Through the same Jesus Christ . . .

The *Libera* is said in a low voice, like the canon, except in the rite of Lyon. The mention of St Andrew is probably due to St Gregory who brought back from Constantinople a large relic and also dedicated to this saint the monastery that he built on the Coelian Hill. Evils past, present and to come refer to sin particularly, but we pray at the same time for temporal peace and preservation from that external and interior disquiet whose effect on Christian life may be formidable.

At the end of the Lord's Prayer the subdeacon takes the paten back to the altar for the fraction. The celebrant takes it during the *Libera*, makes with it a sign of the cross and kisses it before slipping it beneath the host. The origin of the kiss is to be found in the fact that the paten was sometimes used for the kiss of peace. The sign of the cross may formerly have accompanied the conclusion *Per Dominum*; since the fraction has taken this place the sign of the cross was thus put forward.

At this point formerly occurred the solemn episcopal blessings, still in use in Lyon and a few other Churches. They were preceded by a summons to bow down and those who were not going to communicate could then leave. The blessing at nuptial Mass may be a survival of this rite, but it is given between the Lord's Prayer and the *Libera*.

FRACTION, COMMINGLING, KISS OF PEACE

The breaking of the bread mentioned in the account of the Last Supper primitively gave its name to the whole eucharistic rite.[1] It was very necessary and formed a prominent feature when large loaves were consecrated. In order to understand the present ceremonial we must consider again the ancient rite which has already been summarily described in dealing with the Mass at the time of St Gregory.

The *Pax Domini* formed the signal for the kiss of peace which the archdeacon gave to the first among the bishops after kissing the altar or the paten containing the *sancta* of a preceding Mass. Meanwhile the pope made three signs of the cross with his hand over the chalice and, according to one quite plausible view, placed the *sancta* in it: this first commingling was an expression of the moral unity and continuity of sacrifice. But would not the very fact of consuming the *sancta* have been sufficiently symbolical of this? Why place the *sancta* in the chalice? Very possibly it was to make them

[1] See Acts 2. 42; 1 Cor. 10. 16; *Didache* 9. 3.

easier to consume; the altar breads in those days were thick
and soon grew hard and it was useful to moisten them.[1]

On Sundays, the priests of Rome and the neighbourhood
added to the elements that they had consecrated the *fermentum*, a consecrated particle which was sent them by the pope;
they placed it in the chalice at the *Pax Domini*; this rite
emphasized that the Eucharist is preeminently the sacrament
of unity (1 Cor. 10. 17), a fact that Christian antiquity held to
be of such significance that sometimes the Eucharist was sent
as a sign of communion to other bishops, on occasion for
great distances, a practice subsequently forbidden for obvious
reasons of prudence and reverence.

According therefore as to whether it was a papal Mass or
not the commingling was performed with the *sancta* or the
fermentum. This double rite—which has caused not a little
confusion to historians of liturgy—formed a wonderful symbolism of the unity of sacrifice in time and space; it is the
same host which is offered everywhere and always and which
preeminently is the root of the unity of the Church.

After the commingling of the *sancta* the pope broke one of
the consecrated loaves and went to his throne; the portion
that he had broken off remained on the altar until the end
and served as the *sancta* for the next Mass. Then the priests
and the bishops broke the other loaves and placed the pieces
in linen bags which the acolytes wore hanging round their
necks. Meanwhile, after the time of Sergius (beginning of the
eighth century) the *Agnus Dei* was sung.[2] In the tenth century
the custom arose of singing the *Agnus Dei* three times and
adding for the last one "give us peace".

At his throne the pope, as he received the host, broke off
a part of it (with his teeth) and placed it in the chalice saying
a formula not unlike that still to be found in the Missal: this

[1] The Orthodox consecrate on Maundy Thursday for the whole year
the Eucharist reserved for the sick; they sprinkle a little of the
Precious Blood on the consecrated hosts and afterwards dry them.

[2] The *Agnus Dei* does not occur during the Easter Vigil probably
because it was wished to preserve the archaic character of this office.

was the second commingling, the reason for which appears obscure. Recent studies of the *Ordines Romani* lead one to think, however, that after the clergy had communicated from the chalice this particle remaining at the bottom was placed together with the rest of the Precious Blood in a chalice or *scyphus* intended for the people and containing unconsecrated wine; the priests did the same with other particles and other chalices when the number of communicants required it. Until the recent Holy Week reform on Good Friday the celebrant likewise, in performing the fraction, placed a small particle of the consecrated host into the chalice of unconsecrated wine and for long this has been the practice in the east for communion out of Mass. In the early Middle Ages it was believed that in this way a real consecration was effected by contact and that the commingling of the particle of the host with the wine transubstantiated it into the blood of Christ. This teaching is to be found in Amalar's works (ninth century) but it is probably of still earlier date; it spread to various regions and only encountered opposition in the twelfth century when theological statement took a more precise form. Some liturgical books showed traces of it even as late as the sixteenth century; others are silent on the subject or expressly deny it.

In any case, the commingling is a further act of faith in the unity of the sacrament and an assertion that the separation of the body and blood of Christ, realized on the cross, and signified by the double consecration, is apparent only. The commingling is, in addition, a symbol of the resurrection according to the ancient Syrian liturgies and the western medieval rites. And as the resurrection completes the work of the redemption and obtains for us its fruits the term consecration has been applied to the commingling. Obviously, it must be understood in the wide sense of the word, and Mgr Andrieu has shown that it denotes the mingling of a small quantity of wine with the *scyphi* which were to be used for the communion of the faithful.

The fraction was formerly a complicated ceremony in the

Gallican and Mozarabic liturgies, and so it has remained in the eastern liturgies; the particles were arranged in the form of a cross, each symbolizing one of the mysteries of Christ, or even in the form of the human body; an element of superstition was sometimes to be discerned in these practices. At Rome, in the sixth to the eighth centuries, after the celebrant's communion the following station was announced and the noncommunicants were dismissed. In the light of the foregoing the present rites can more easily be explained.

The first commingling, that of the *sancta* or *fermentum*, has disappeared and the second has taken the place of the first with the difference that it takes place at the *Pax Domini*; as a result the fraction is anticipated during the conclusion of the *Libera*. The kiss of peace no longer accompanies the formula *Pax Domini* as would seem obvious, but has been postponed after the *Agnus Dei* and a preparatory prayer. A certain dislocation therefore has occurred at this point of the Mass and Dom Capelle has proposed[1] a simple rearrangement which would restore agreement between words and ceremonies. According to this the *Libera* would be said aloud, as always in the Lyon rite and in the Roman rite on Good Friday. The prayer *Domine Jesu Christe* for peace would come immediately afterwards, followed by the *Pax Domini* and the kiss of peace. The celebrant would then kiss the paten (in silence) and perform the fraction and commingling. Meanwhile the choir would sing the *Agnus Dei* which would thus return to its primitive position; at low Mass the priest would say it after the fraction and commingling.

The fraction takes place at present, therefore, at the end of the *Libera* and is hardly noticeable by the congregation, the use of unleavened bread having restricted it to the celebrant's host. He breaks this into three parts: with the smallest he makes three signs of the cross over the chalice saying the *Pax Domini*: "May the peace of the Lord be always with you." Then he drops this particle into the chalice saying:

[1] *Revue bénédictine*, 1941, pp. 5–40.

"May this sacramental commingling of the body and blood of our Lord Jesus Christ be for us who receive it a source of eternal life. Amen."

One of the two remaining particles was formerly used as the *sancta* for another Mass, and then as *viaticum* for the dying; the other was intended for the celebrant's communion. Nowadays he receives both.

The *Agnus Dei* ("Lamb of God, who takest away the sins of the world, have mercy on us"—at the third repetition, "give us peace") is no longer a chant during the fraction and acts as an introduction to the kiss of peace. As a threefold invocation of the Lamb who was slain and a threefold act of faith in his presence it is admirably placed at this point as a preparation for communion. Originally it was sung to a very simple melody; this still remains at Mass for the dead and during penitential seasons. In the Middle Ages many melodies, as numerous and varied as those for the *Sanctus*, were composed for the *Agnus Dei*. They are remarkable for the impression of urgent prayer and great recollection that they produce.

The kiss of peace is a further prelude to the communion. This symbol of charity and union goes back to the first days of the Church : St Paul bears witness to its use in four of his epistles (Rom. 16 : 16; 1 Cor. 16. 20; 2 Cor. 13. 12; 1 Thess. 5. 26). The oriental and Gallican liturgies placed it at the end of the Mass of the catechumens, before the offertory, perhaps in reminiscence of the passage in Matthew (5. 23–4) which requires reconciliation with our enemies before bringing our gift to the altar. At the time of Innocent I, Rome and Africa made the kiss of peace an obligatory prelude to communion, thus carrying into effect the petition of the Lord's Prayer "Forgive us our trespasses as we forgive them that trespass against us".

The kiss of peace is introduced by a prayer said by the celebrant bowing low and looking at the host :

Lord Jesus Christ, who didst say to thy apostles : I leave

peace with you; it is my own peace that I give you: look not upon my sins but upon thy Church's faith, and deign to give her peace and unity in accordance with thy will: thou who art God, living and reigning for ever and ever. Amen.

The priest kisses the altar, so to say receiving therefrom the peace of Christ. He then imparts it to the deacon, the deacon to the subdeacon and the latter to the rest of the clergy. Each in giving the embrace says "Peace be with you". Both formula and gesture varied in the past. Often the celebrant kissed the Missal and the host. Until the eighth century all present took part in the rite, men and women separately. In the thirteenth century the embrace was substituted for the kiss with the mouth. At a Mass without deacon and subdeacon on certain occasions a plaque (known as a pax-board or pax brede: it is made of metal or ivory and used to be richly ornamented) is passed round to be kissed. Still nowadays in some places a pax brede is presented to be kissed at nuptial and funeral Masses.

The connection between the kiss of peace and the communion is also expressed in the kiss given to the papal or episcopal ring before receiving the host. The *Ceremonial of Bishops* also lays down that the deacon and subdeacon when they communicate should kiss the hand and cheek of the prelate. Romano Guardini[1] aptly remarks that our kiss of peace is "a masterpiece of reserve, behaviour and distinction". The faithful, although they are now only spectators of the rite, should not forget the implied lesson in Christian brotherhood and unity in the mystical body.

THE COMMUNION

The sacrificial meal naturally includes the eating of the victim by all those taking part in it. Communion by the priest who celebrates is an absolute rule. But the desire of the Church, recalled in the sixteenth century by the Council of Trent, is that the faithful should communicate whenever they hear

[1] *The Spirit of the Liturgy*, Sheed & Ward, London and New York.

Mass. This desire is being increasingly realized by fervent Catholics since the decrees of Pius X on the communion of children and on daily communion. Participation in Mass without communicating is incomplete and, in a word, abnormal, although strictly speaking the law of the Church requires only the Easter communion. Pius XII's Encyclical *Mediator* even requires that, so far as possible, hosts consecrated during the actual Mass at which they are present should be given to the faithful thus emphasizing admirably the connection between the communion and the sacrifice.

Since the fourteenth century the immediate preparation consists of two prayers of Gallican origin, private prayers selected from many others and retained by our Missal. The first is of imposing theological inspiration recalling the anamnesis:

> Lord Jesus Christ, Son of the living God, who by the Father's will and the cooperation of the Holy Spirit, didst by thy death bring life to the world, deliver me by this most holy Body and Blood of thine from all my sins and from every evil. Make me always cling to thy commandments, and never allow me to be parted from thee: who with the selfsame God the Father and the Holy Spirit art God, living and reigning for ever and ever. Amen.

This prayer, which contemplates Christ in his glory and in his sacramental presence, like that which follows, is directed to be said by the celebrant as he looks at the host; it is a small detail, but a revealing one of the devotional inspiration of which the prayer is redolent.

The final prayer is a humble avowal of unworthiness and a last petition for purification, so that the reception of the Eucharist should not be the cause of our condemnation. It mentions only our Lord's body, and thus it alone is retained on Good Friday when communion is received under the species of bread only:

> Let not the partaking of thy body, Lord Jesus Christ, which I, unworthy as I am, make bold to receive, turn against me

into judgement and damnation, but through thy loving kindness let it be for me a safeguard of mind and body, and in it
let me find healing; thou who art God, living and reigning with
God the Father in the unity of the Holy Spirit, world without
end. Amen.

The priest then takes the host and, before communicating,
repeats three times the wonderful invocation of the centurion
at Capharnaum (Matt. 8. 8), of which only one word is
changed: "Lord, I am not worthy that thou shouldst enter
beneath my roof, but say only the word, and my soul shall be
healed."

He signs himself with the host and consumes it saying:
"The body of our Lord Jesus Christ preserve my soul for
everlasting life. Amen."

He pauses for a moment in recollection, recites two verses
from the psalms and communicates from the chalice saying a
similar formula.

The communion of the faithful then follows, and this is
its normal place, during the sacrifice. The custom prevalent
in some places of invariably giving communion outside Mass
when there is no legitimate reason for doing so, is greatly
to be deplored. A final preparation is the recitation of the
Confiteor (with one or two exceptions in the Holy Week rites);
the priest adds *Misereatur* and *Indulgentiam*. Then, holding
up a host, he says: "Behold the Lamb of God, behold him
who takes away the sins of the world." He repeats thrice for
the faithful the *Domine non sum dignus* and communicates
them saying for each: "The body of our Lord Jesus Christ
preserve your soul for everlasting life."

The *Confiteor* and the rest have been taken over from the
order of communion outside Mass provided by the Ritual.
The holding up of the host and the reference to the Lamb as
the Redeemer at this point are evocative: the centurion's
humble request also is here very much to the point together
with the wish, inspired by our Lord's discourse on the bread

of life (John 6) that the body of Christ may preserve the souls of the communicants for everlasting life.

The communion was preceded in the early centuries by an admonition from the deacon: "Holy things for holy people!" followed by an order that those who were not going to communicate should retire. The faithful received under both kinds, the pope or bishop giving the host and a deacon the chalice. Each communicant answered *Amen* to the short formula of administration: "The body of Christ—the blood of Christ, the chalice of life." The Eucharist was received standing, except perhaps on fast days. When the altar breads came to be made very thin they were placed in the communicants' mouths and not in their right hand, and since then communion has been received kneeling, a practice that, given modern notions on the subject, is certainly more reverent.

The following instructions by St Cyril of Jerusalem are redolent of the devotion of the early Church:

> Therefore in approaching come not with wrists extended or fingers open; but make your left hand a throne for the right which is about to receive the King. And having hollowed your palm, receive the body of Christ, saying after it, Amen. Then, after carefully hallowing your eyes with the touch of the holy body, partake of it, being careful not to lose any of it; for what you lose is a loss for you as if it were one of your own limbs . . . Then, having partaken of the Body of Christ, approach also to the chalice of his blood; not stretching forth your hands, but, bowing in worship and reverence, say Amen and be sanctified by partaking of the blood of Christ. And while your lips are still moist with it, touching it with your hands sanctify your eyes, brow and other senses. Then wait for the prayer and thank God who has accounted you worthy of so great mysteries.[1]

At Rome the higher clergy received a particle from the pope's host; each carried it to the altar, on which he placed his hand before communicating, then went to sip from the pope's chalice presented by one of the assistants. Into all the

[1] *Mystagogical Catecheses*, 5. 21 *seq.*

chalices were poured a few drops from the pope's chalice in order to emphasize once more the symbolism of unity.

After the eighth century communion from the chalice was received by means of a tube or reed. Intinction, which consists of dipping the host in the chalice, was only practised in the east, where it is still the custom, but it never took root in the west where it seems to have aroused a certain repugnance, since for communion given in this way a spoon was used. Nowadays the Greeks in union with Rome are more apt to dip the host in the chalice without letting it out of the hand.

In the west the giving of communion under the species of wine had become rare by the twelfth century and was finally abolished by the Council of Constance in 1415. This decision was the final stage in a long evolutionary process which increasingly restricted the use of the chalice by the laity. At an early date in Rome ordinary wine, with which a few drops of consecrated wine had been mingled, was administered to them; in fact only one chalice was placed on the altar and this alone was consecrated in order to show clearly the unity of the mystical body and also to reproduce as exactly as possible the Last Supper. This chalice was probably not very large, for the archdeacon moved it about on several occasions during Mass. It must have been insufficient directly the faithful became at all numerous. Elsewhere, wine was added to the chalice when the precious blood began to diminish, or, as has been described above in connection with the commingling, the wine administered to the faithful was "sanctified" by a consecrated particle.

Communion from the chalice held also certain drawbacks. There was the danger of spilling it; it was difficult to estimate the amount of wine required and to reserve any of the precious blood remaining over, especially in hot climates where the eucharistic accidents were in danger of corrupting or turning sour very quickly. The scarcity of wine in northern countries may have influenced development in like manner. In addition, Christian antiquity never regarded communion under both kinds as an absolute principle; it was given under one kind only (from the chalice) to small children; for prisoners, the dying, and communion in private houses the host alone was reserved. Finally in the twelfth century with the development of theology it was made quite clear that Christ is present whole and entire under each kind—the living and immortal Christ whose passion is recalled by the sacramental words but whose body and blood cannot be separated. This change in the discipline concerning the chalice took place gradually without arousing any protest save in the fifteenth century among the Hussites in Bohemia whom the Church was obliged to condemn at the Council of Constance, for not only did they demand the restoration of the chalice to the laity but termed what had become the common practice heretical and sacrilegious. The way for the withdrawal of the chalice had been prepared by the liturgical developments in connection with the host such as the elevation, the desire to see the host, worship paid to the reserved Eucharist and the Corpus Christi procession.

Until the fourth century the people communicated at every Mass and on those days on which Mass was not celebrated they communicated at home. After the peace of the Church, and especially from the ninth century onwards, communion became increasingly rare until in 1215 the Council of the Lateran sanctioned the minimum of an annual Easter communion which many probably had no intention of exceeding. How is that regrettable state of affairs to be explained? Its causes appear to be very complex. Among others may be mentioned the influx into the Church of superficial and slack Christians, the severity of penitential discipline and the eucharistic fast and even the development in the Middle Ages of devotion to the Blessed Sacrament, one of the effects of which was the practice of "spiritual communion", an act of faith joined with the desire for sacramental communion. Too often, even in our own day, the faithful are satisfied with this; nevertheless spiritual communion is far better than passive, more or less indifferent presence at Mass.

COMMUNION AND THANKSGIVING

In the fourth century during the communion a psalm with an antiphon was sung, as at the introit and offertory. Psalms 22 (*Dominus regit me*, "The Lord is my shepherd") and 33 (*Benedicam Dominum*, "At all times I will bless the Lord"), certain verses of which could be taken as referring to the Eucharist, were favourites; otherwise the introit psalm was repeated. Between the tenth and twelfth centuries the psalm practically disappeared, and nowadays in the Missal as with the offertory chant we have no more than the former refrain, that is, the antiphon. In addition the singing of the communion is postponed until after all have communicated, for the fraction is over in a moment and the *Agnus Dei* fills in the intervening period. The present increase in communion arouses the hope that the singing of the antiphon will be restored to the point at which the faithful are going up to the altar; in some churches this has been done and the recent reformed rite for Holy Week on Maundy Thursday and Good Friday appoints psalms and antiphons which may be sung at this time.

The communion anthem is ordinarily taken from the psalms. During the weeks of Lent the order of the psalter is followed beginning with psalm 1 on Ash Wednesday, except for the Masses on the Thursday, which are of late introduction, and some others. The antiphon is sometimes taken from other books of the Old Testament or the New; very rarely it is an ecclesiastical composition. Obviously, the words have frequently no connection with the Eucharist.

The chant to which the communion anthem is set has become progressively more ornate, as is the case with the other chanted portions of the Mass propers. The Gregorian composers appear to have enjoyed a free hand and some of their musical adaptations, which show great variety, are masterpieces. Among many others we may draw attention to those of the second Sunday after Epiphany and of the Saturday after the second Sunday of Lent, which are almost syllabic chants, to the simple and unostentatiously rhythmical chants of the

Christmas midnight Mass and of Low Sunday and the solemn and imposing chant for Easter Sunday.

THE ABLUTIONS

After the communion of the faithful the priest takes two ablutions. The first is intended to purify with a small quantity of wine the celebrant's mouth and the chalice. The second consists in pouring over his fingers wine and water which he then consumes. The rite is a natural one and certainly very ancient, though it has varied a good deal in its details. In addition at a pontifical Mass the bishop washes his hands and many priests do so on their return to the sacristy. Attacks on the doctrine of the real presence probably contributed to the development of these precautions and marks of respect.

Two ancient prayers form the accompaniment of the ablutions. One, *Quod ore sumpsimus,* probably goes back to the fourth century and is used as the postcommunion on the Thursday after Passion Sunday. The priest asks that "what we have received with our mouths we may possess in purity of mind; and may the gift of the moment become for us an everlasting remedy". The second prayer, *Corpus tuum,* of Gallican origin, was at first a prayer of private devotion; in it the celebrant prays that the body and blood of Christ may "cleave to every fibre" of his being and that as a result of the reception of this sacrament no stain of sin may be left in him. All these detailed prescriptions were made obligatory by Pius V's Missal. A rite analogous to the ablutions was instituted for the faithful when communion under both kinds was no longer the practice; they were given a small quantity of wine as an aid to consume the host. This practice has been dropped for a long time past, and now survives only at ordination Masses.

POSTCOMMUNION

After these silent prayers there follows the solemn thanksgiving, or postcommunion; this is the final prayer, *ad com-*

plendam, corresponding to the collect and the secret. It is necessary to thank God for the graces received, as our Saviour himself with his apostles sang the psalms of the Hallel after the Last Supper (Matt. 26. 30). This thought of gratitude forms the inspiration of the final prayer; there is often added to it a petition asking that the effect of the sacrament may endure in the souls of the recipients together with a short reference to the feast of the day or the liturgical season. The greeting *Dominus vobiscum* is now made real in its highest sense: the Lord *is* with the faithful if, as the postcommunions usually take for granted, the congregation has communicated.

In the postcommunions we encounter once again the characteristic features of the Roman collects—a restrained style and an unobtrusive and quietly lyrical quality. They are often very fine indeed and from them could be compiled a theology of the effects of the Eucharist—graces for the soul, increase of theological virtues, gifts and fruits of the Holy Spirit, a remedy for the body, the unity of the mystical body, eternal life. The expressions used (heavenly food, life-giving food, heavenly mystery, spiritual food, reception of the body and blood of Christ) state formally or equivalently the doctrine of the real presence. The examples which follow illustrate this general tendency.

Ember Friday in Advent

May the holy receiving of thy sacrament, Lord, give us new strength, purge us of our old selves, and bring us into closer union with the life-giving Mystery.

Christmas Eve

Grant, Lord, that we, who find meat and drink in the heavenly sacrament thy only-begotten Son has given us, may draw the breath of new life in rehearsing his nativity.

Christmas Day (third Mass)

Almighty God, we pray thee grant that the Saviour of the world, whose birth on this day has brought about our own rebirth in godliness, may also bestow on us immortal life.

Baptism of our Lord (January 13th)

Let thy heavenly light shine always and everywhere before us, Lord, so that we may have clear vision to discern, and fitting dispositions to receive, the sacrament of which thou hast willed us to partake.

Sixth Sunday after Epiphany

Grant, Lord, that we who have feasted at thy heavenly banquet may ever hunger after the true bread of life.

Fourth Wednesday in Lent

May thy heavenly banquet, Lord, of which we have partaken, sanctify us, purify us from all errors, and so make us worthy of the divine promises.

Fourth Saturday in Lent

We beg thee, almighty God, that we may be counted among his members of whose body and blood we have partaken.

Maundy Thursday

Strengthened by the bread of life, we pray thee, Lord our God, that our strivings in this mortal life may win us everlasting life with thee.

Easter Sunday

Pour into us the Spirit of thy love, O Lord, so that we whose hunger thou hast satisfied with thy Easter sacraments may, by thy loving kindness, be made one in heart.

Low Sunday

We pray thee, Lord our God, that the sacred rites thou hast bestowed upon us to safeguard this new life of ours may bring us healing now and in time to come.

Whit Tuesday

May the Holy Spirit heal our souls with the divine sacrament, we beseech thee, Lord, for he is himself the remission of all sins.

Corpus Christi

Grant us, Lord, we beseech thee, through all eternity that enjoyment of thy godhead which is foreshadowed in this life by our partaking of thy precious body and blood.

Eleventh Sunday after Pentecost

May thy sacrament of which we have partaken, Lord, be felt by us as a support for mind and body, so that, having health in both, we may glory in the fullness of divine healing.

SS. Peter and Paul (June 29th)

Let the pleading of thy apostles move thee, Lord, to keep from all adversity those whom thou hast filled with the bread of heaven.

These restrained prayers of thanksgiving are sufficiently general in nature to be suitable for all and so expressed as to leave freedom to the Holy Spirit to act as he will in souls. It would be an excellent idea to use them as inspiration for personal prayer during the course of the day. If we are able to understand them properly they will call us by the voice of the Church to dwell on our sharing in the life of Christ rather than on the personal benefit to ourselves, though in reality the two things are inseparable; in one sense, it is less Christ who enters into us and rather we who enter into him and into his life.

PRAYER OVER THE PEOPLE

On weekdays in Lent a further prayer is added at this point preceded by an admonition from the deacon: *Humiliate capita vestra Deo*, "Bow down your heads before God". In fact it is a form of blessing which concerns all present and not only those who have communicated. Formerly it was said at all Masses, as can be seen from the Leonine sacramentary, and it is not known how it came to be reserved to the week-days of Lent. The most probable explanation is that St Gregory made it into a blessing for public penitents with whom the rest of the congregation associated themselves, although these prayers exhibit no particular penitential character. In style they are closely allied to the collects. In addition to the conclusion of Mass they are used also as the collect for Vespers, except on Saturdays. The following are two examples of the prayer over the people.

Friday after Ash Wednesday

Protect thy people, Lord, and mercifully wash all their sins away, for if no wickedness hold sway in them, no enemy shall hurt them.

Ember Wednesday in Lent

Enlighten our minds, we pray thee, Lord, by the brightness of thy shining, so that we may be able to see what we should do, and have the strength to do it.

THE DISMISSAL

There now remains only the dismissal of the congregation (*missa* in Latin). It is done, somewhat coldly, by the deacon whose office is to give instructions to the faithful in the celebrant's name. *Ite, missa est* means simply "Go, this is the dismissal". Some well-intentioned modern authors who explain the sense of this instruction as if it meant "Go, now your mission is beginning" are stating an idea that in itself is certainly correct, but in so doing manifest their ignorance of liturgical Latin. Well-founded advice can be given to the faithful without basing it on a mistranslation.

When the *Gloria* has not been said, for *Ite, missa est* is substituted *Benedicamus Domino*, "Let us bless the Lord". It is difficult to explain the reason for this. Perhaps *Ite, missa est* was given a rather joyful interpretation which tended to exclude it on penitential days; or else, since formerly the *Gloria* was reserved to the bishop, *Ite, missa est* was linked with it implying an idea of authority. The formula of dismissal is sung with some solemnity to the melody used for the *Kyrie*. The congregation answers, to the same tune, *Deo gratias*, "Thanks be to God". At Masses for the dead *Requiescant in pace* ("May they rest in peace") is said. Very properly the present Mass for Maundy Thursday, when it is followed by the procession to the altar of repose, concludes with *Benedicamus Domino*, since the congregation is not immediately dismissed.

FINAL PRAYERS

It would seem natural to leave the altar at once, but the celebrant says a prayer, *Placeat*, in which he asks the Holy Trinity to accept the sacrifice and to make it fruitful for himself and for those for whose intention he has offered it.

He then kisses the altar; this forms his farewell to the holy table as it did his first mark of respect at the beginning of Mass. Then he blesses the faithful with the well-known formula, "Almighty God bless you: the Father, the Son and the Holy Ghost", and he makes the sign of the cross over them. A bishop's blessing is preceded by two versicles and responses from the psalms and includes a threefold sign of the cross. The blessing is omitted from Masses of the dead in which many of the more solemn ceremonies are also absent. Formerly the blessing was sometimes given with the paten, a chalice or a cross. The present rite, like all the secondary elements that we have encountered, was fixed by Pius V.

Since about the thirteenth century the blessing has been followed by the reading, without solemnity, of the prologue of the Gospel of St John (1. 1–14). The people, who had great devotion to this magnificent passage, used to ask for it to be read aloud at the altar and Pius V made it obligatory. Before this it was often said during the procession to the sacristy or else on arrival there. At pontifical Mass it is said as the bishop leaves the altar. It is now omitted from the solemn offices on Palm Sunday, Maundy Thursday and the Easter vigil. In some places it is said over the newly baptized and the Ritual suggests it, with other passages from the Gospels, for visits to the sick.

The prayers after Mass have not been inserted in the Missal and are of a temporary nature. Leo XIII ordered them in order to obtain a solution to the Roman question. Since the Lateran Treaty they are said for Russia. They are omitted after sung Masses and after those celebrated with a certain solemnity (nuptial Masses, for example).

As a final thanksgiving on his way to the sacristy, or after unvesting, the celebrant recites privately the canticle of the children in the fiery furnace (Dan. 3. 57–90, *passim*) and psalm 150 followed by some versicles and three collects. The Missal also proposes for optional use two other prayers the first of which, a very ancient one, is attributed to St Thomas Aquinas and the other is by St Bonaventure. A private, silent thanksgiving is highly desirable for all those who have communicated; it forms a fitting complement of private prayer after public worship and is an authentic expression of devotion. It is emphatically recommended in Pius XII's encyclical on the liturgy (*Mediator*).

CONCLUSION

Those who usually frequent low Mass may possibly have expressed some surprise that in the course of this book constant reference has been made to high Mass and even to Mass celebrated solemnly by a bishop or the pope. In fact papal or pontifical Mass, gathering the Christian community around its head, is the primitive form of liturgical celebration; this will be readily understood when it is remembered that at one period Christianity was principally concentrated in the towns, and each city, even each village of any importance, had its own bishop. All the ceremonial has grown up in close connection with this state of affairs. The spread of Christianity into the country districts and the foundation of monasteries led to simpler forms of celebration which were Mass sung by a priest assisted by a deacon and subdeacon, Mass sung by a priest without sacred ministers, and lastly, low Mass, often called, though wrongly, private Mass. When a priest celebrates alone he adds to his functions those of the deacon and subdeacon so that the rules which he follows may be regarded as a reduction of high or pontifical Mass.

High Mass and the parochial sung Mass should be the form preferred by the faithful if they have understood the fundamentally communal, collective nature of the Mass and the duty of actively taking part in it which is obviously easier of realization at a high rather than at a low Mass. In those places where high Mass has been made into a real manifestation of public community worship with the congregation taking their proper part it has resulted in great spiritual benefits and a deepening of Christian life. The practice of dialogue Mass can also offer similar advantages. What is essential is for the people to unite themselves to the priest, to pray and offer with him instead of isolating themselves in their individual, private prayers, which of course have their worth but would be more in place before or after the holy sacrifice. Joyfully we must join in the great current of the Church's prayer, even if it means giving up old, long-cherished habits. The present liturgical revival, if it results in making this practice of prayer in common a general one, will, on this score alone, have borne abundant fruit.

*   *   *

In spite of the succinctness and austerity of the liturgical formulas it is impossible not to be struck by the great spiritual riches of the Mass. Its aspects are many and varied as are the lessons to be derived from it. As a conclusion to this short book it will not be unprofitable to summarize what have been called the essential features of the Mass.

The notion of sacrifice is fundamental to it. The Mass is primarily the memorial of the passion; in an unbloody manner it continues the sacrifice of Calvary, by applying to us its effects, with the repetition of the Last Supper following our Saviour's command. Christ makes himself present on the altar; he carries on there the offering that he made of himself for the salvation of the world at the Last Supper and on the cross which he ever continues to make in heaven. This is a mysterious reality; its existence is guaranteed by the twofold consecration and it is indeed a true sacrifice. By the ministry of the priest Christ effects what he himself did before giving himself up to death. Then he offered in advance his sacrifice with the shedding of blood on the cross; now that this has been accomplished he orders his Church to renew the oblation of it under the appearances of bread and wine. The simultaneous presence of these two elements and the consecratory words are a striking reminder that his body and blood were separated on the cross. Now they are no longer separated, any more than they were at the Last Supper. Christ is wholly present under each kind; the indissoluble link between the Mass and the passion is clearly brought out. As St Paul said, the Lord's death is announced, is heralded (1 Cor. 11. 26). And as it is the risen Christ, immortal and glorified, who is present under the sacramental species, the resurrection and ascension are commemorated at the same time as the passion. St Thomas could say that the whole mystery of our salvation is here present at the same time, and this is the meaning of the prayer *Unde et memores.*

The Mass, Christ's sacrifice offered by the Church, is also the Church's sacrifice. The purpose of every sacrificial offering is the gift of self to God and the external expression of this gift by the giving up of what is offered and renunciation of its use. At Mass, the offering, materially, is very modest, but it is of high significance for bread and wine are the stay of our bodily life and in a certain manner represent this life itself.

The Church's sacrifice starts at the beginning of Mass with the prayers and lessons arranged with the purpose of arousing in the soul repentance and self oblation. It assumes external shape when the bread and wine are brought to the altar. This provisional offering takes on definitive form in the consecration which transforms it into what is most sacred in the whole world and, by virtue of this transformation, makes manifest its acceptance by God.

With this divine acceptance there should correspond the effective sacrifice of the Church and of all her members by a renewed effort of identification with Christ's adorable dispositions in his passion, by obedience and surrender to God, by perfect love of God and of our neighbour. The Church's sacrifice, in progress since the beginning of Mass, receives at the consecration its divine seal; but for God to receive it as pleasing to him, and for this sacrifice to have real significance, the members of the Church must enter into Christ's passion and give themselves up to God in all the generosity of their heart and in a spirit of entire surrender. Thus they will show the sincerity of their dispositions and be enabled, in the same measure, to share in the fruits of redemption, in the gift of divine life which the risen Christ pours out on those who have real love for him, for the cross is not laid upon us for its own sake: it leads to life and glory.

Since, by our Saviour's will, our sacrifice assumes the form of a sacred meal it is normally completed by partaking of the divine Victim. Is it not strange that often the celebrant alone communicates? Inevitably one's thoughts turn to the parable of the refused invitations and the poor excuses offered by the guests summoned to the royal banquet. A better understanding of the Mass should lead to a desire for the Eucharist, for reception of it implies not only the visit of Christ, "the living bread come down from heaven" of great profit to our souls, but the privileged means of being united to his sacrifice, by acceptance of our daily cross, by the practice of fraternal charity, by a deepening of the sentiment of the unity of the Church of which the participation by all in the eucharistic bread is both its most perfect symbol and its most effective means: "The one bread makes us one body, though we are many in number; the same bread is shared by all" (1 Cor. 10. 17).

Christian antiquity, as the primitive forms of the anaphora have made clear for us, emphasized particularly the thanksgiving and praise of God rather than the sacrifice. It is a difference of emphasis merely, for thanksgiving, which is one of the dominant themes of the Mass, cannot remain on an abstract and ineffective level. It turns to action and is expressed by the gift offered to God of the body and blood of our Saviour which presupposes the offering and gift of ourselves and the Church. All is harmoniously combined in gratitude, thanksgiving and praise for the redemptive sacrifice of Christ in the mystical renewal of this sacrifice and by the participation of all in the dispositions that it requires. It is by joining ourselves to the sacrifice of Jesus Christ through the holy oblation of the Mass, continued in a life marked by the cross, that we really give thanks to God, honour and praise to the Father by the Son, in the unity of the Holy Spirit: "Each and every offering of this memorial sacrifice carries on the work of our redemption" (Secret, ninth Sunday after Pentecost).

SELECT BIBLIOGRAPHY

JUNGMANN, Joseph Andreas, S.J.: *The Mass of the Roman Rite, its Origins and Development* (Missarum Solemnia) translated by F. A. Brunner, C.SS.R. Two Volumes. New York, Benziger, 1951 and 1955. (This authoritative and exhaustive work contains a complete bibliography on all aspects of the liturgy of the Mass.)

BAUMSTARK, Anton: *Comparative Liturgy*, revised by Bernard Botte, O.S.B., translated by F. L. Cross, Mowbray, London, and Newman Press, Westminster, Md, 1958.

KLAUSER, Theodor: *The Western Liturgy*, translated by F. L. Cross, Mowbray, London, 1952.

Translations of the *Didache*, the Epistles of Clement of Rome, Ignatius of Antioch, etc., will be found in the *Ancient Christian Writers* series, Volumes 1 and 6, Longmans, London, and Newman Press, Westminster, Md.

CROSS, F. L. (Editor): *St. Cyril of Jerusalem's Lectures on the Christian Sacraments* (The Procathesis and the five mystagogical Catecheses). S.P.C.K., London, and Macmillan, New York, 1951.

CROEGAERT, A.: *The Mass, a Liturgical Commentary.* Two volumes, translated and abridged by J. Holland-Smith, Burns Oates, London, and Newman Press, Westminster, Md, 1958–59.

FELTOE, C. L.: *Sacramentarium leonianum,* Cambridge Univ. Press, 1906.

WILSON, H. A.: *The Gelasian Sacramentary*, Oxford Univ. Press, 1894.

WILSON, H.A.: *The Gregorian Sacramentary under Charles the Great.* Harrison and Sons, London (for the Henry Bradshaw Society), 1915.

CHERY, H., O.P.: *What is the Mass?* Translated by Lancelot C. Sheppard, Blackfriars, London, and Newman Press, Westminster, Md, 1953.

ROGUET, A. M., O.P.: *Holy Mass, Approaches to the Mystery*, Blackfriars, London, 1953.

MURPHY, John L.: *The Mass and the Liturgical Reform*, Bruce, Milwaukee, 1957.

GUARDINI, Romano: *The Spirit of the Liturgy*, Sheed and Ward, London and New York, 1939.

TRETHOWAN, Illtyd, *Christ in the Liturgy*. Sheed and Ward, London and New York, 1952.

Mediator Dei et Hominum. On the Sacred Liturgy (Encyclical Letter of Pius XII). Edited with notes by Gerard Ellard, S.J., New York, America Press, 1948. Another edition, translated by Mgr G. Smith, Catholic Truth Society, London, 1948.

DANIEL-ROPS, Henri, *This is the Mass* Translated by Alastair Guinan, celebrated by Fulton J. Sheen, photographed by Yousuf Karsh, with an introduction by Bishop Sheen, Hawthorn Books, New York, 1958.